Garry Nicholas

WJEC
GCSE
Drama
Unit 1 Devised Practical Performance

Published in 2013 by Illuminate Publishing Ltd, P.O. Box 1160, Cheltenham, Gloucestershire GL50 9RW

Orders: please visit www.illuminatepublishing.com or email sales@illuminatepublishing.com

British Library Cataloguing in Publication Data

A catalogue record for this book is available from the British Library

ISBN 978-1-908682-19-2

Printed by Ashford Colour Press Ltd, Gosport, Hampshire

Date of publication: 09.13

The Publisher's policy is to use papers that are natural, renewable and recyclable products made from wood grown in sustainable forests. The logging and manufacturing processes are expected to conform to the environmental regulations of the country of origin.

Every effort has been made to contact copyright holders of material produced in this book. If notified, the publisher will be pleased to rectify any errors or omissions at the earliest opportunity.

This material has been endorsed by WJEC and offers high quality support for the delivery of WJEC qualifications. While this material has been through a WJEC quality assurance process, all responsibility for the content remains with the publisher.

Editor: Geoff Tuttle
Design & layout: emc design ltd

Contents

This book is designed to help you to get to grips with **Unit 1: The Devised Practical Performance** of your GCSE Drama course. In it you are expected to devise and perform your own scene. The book is divided into five sections: Devising, Theatre Practitioners, Theatre Genres, How to Perform and How to Evaluate.

Think of this book as a guide that will take you on a journey – it can help you step by step from the starting line, where you will devise your scene using a particular practitioner or genre, through to performing the scene and to the finish line, where you will write an evaluation of your devised performance.

This book will be your **devising toolkit.**

It will help you to fix any problems you may have when devising your own scene. Problems such as:

- How to interpret the theme effectively.
- How to show an in-depth understanding of your role.
- How to use movement and space in a disciplined manner.
- How to engage the audience.

This toolkit will have all the tools to help you with these issues such as: using dramatic devices, tips on how to perform effectively and sustain audience interest completely throughout the entire performance.

You will learn about three theatre practitioners – about their ideas for the theatre, about their techniques and how to incorporate these ideas into your own work. The Practitioners are Brecht, Augusto Boal and Stanislavski seen here in that order from left clockwise.

There are three theatre genres for you to consider:

- Physical Theatre
- Theatre in Education
- Musical Theatre.

Which one will you choose to base your devised scene on? Not sure? Then this toolkit will help you decide!

You will also learn about how to perform your own devised scene and discover tips and hints to get the best marks possible from the examiner. This book will give you direction and advice on how to ensure that your own individual performance is effective and engaging.

Tips like the following:

To learn more go to Section 4.

The final section – Evaluation – is very important. This helps you to develop a skill which examiners often feel is one of the weakest areas they see from student performances. This is the skill of writing an evaluation of your own performance in your devised scene. In this book you'll find plenty of guidance to take you step by step through the process of writing your evaluation, and give you an example of a model evaluation to consider.

Read, enjoy and learn from your devising toolkit – and who knows, at the end of it all, this might be you ...

HOW DO I DEVISE?

WHAT WILL I LEARN?

- What we mean when we talk about devising in drama, and why it is important
- Examples of how devices can help you when considering how to devise your scene

What is devising? Well put simply, it is the term used for creating a piece of original drama – in other words, making up your own scenes!

Steps to successful devising

There are perhaps **FIVE** main steps that you should be aware of that are at the heart of all successful devised scenes in theatre, drama companies or performers.

1 Listen to all ideas

Listening to everyone's individual suggestions is a great approach to take because if you listen fairly and equally to all the ideas from the people you're working with – and if you allow everyone to feel able to put forward their own view – then you will end up having more material to work with.

2 Keep an open mind

When you start devising, you can never be sure what the outcome will be, so it is very important to stay positive and open-minded. Plus you'll find this helps you keep your focus when things go wrong or you do not feel that things are going anywhere.

3 Have a clear objective

TOP TIP!

Groups of four or five normally work best for devising as there are enough people to create interesting scenarios and not too many to make teamwork difficult.

It is important to always remember to have a clear objective for each lesson. Why is this so important? Well, if you do not do this, then it becomes all too easy for people to get distracted and side-tracked by losing interest in the project. This is even more the case if you happen to have group members who don't feel like they are doing anything worthwhile.

4 Co-operate as a team

You need to work together so that the whole team can give ideas, and no idea gets thrown aside. If you do not work as a team, people can feel excluded and left out. The more people work together in the team, then the more ideas you can work on and usually you'll end up with a much better and more valuable outcome.

5 Keep positive

Perhaps the most difficult of all the steps to bear in mind, but it is crucial to have a positive outlook and attitude when in the devising process. Nothing else helps to create a positive and friendly atmosphere for creating a healthy working environment as much as remaining upbeat in your outlook.

Who uses devised work in the theatre?

COMPLICITE
Founded in 1983 by Simon McBurney, Annabel Arden, and Marcello Magni.

Complicite's work has ranged from entirely devised work to theatrical adaptations and revivals of classic texts.

MIKE LEIGH
Born in Salford, Manchester, in 1943, Mike Leigh has developed a unique method of creating films and plays through controlled **improvisations.**

KNEEHIGH
Kneehigh Theatre is an international theatre company based in Cornwall, England. They use a variety of theatrical elements including puppetry, live music and an emphasis on visual imagery.

IMPROBABLE
Improbable Theatre is a UK theatre company founded in 1996. The company took theatre-making in new directions with a mix of puppetry, improvisation, comedy and storytelling, transforming the unlikeliest of material into striking entertainment.

Using games for devising

1 Whose shoes?

A game exploring the links between costume, physicality and characterisation.

TIP
These words are defined in the Glossary.

How to play

This game is incredibly simple and rewarding. Place a box in the middle of the room, and fill it with assorted shoes; the more varied the better. It is possible for the pupils to bring in a couple of pairs each if they wish.

The players should sit facing the playing space. One by one, players should go up, moving in a neutral fashion, and peer inside the box. They must then take out a shoe. When they put this shoe on, that side of their body becomes inhabited by the shoe's character. For instance, a high heel might give you a feminine, alluring model; a thick-soled black shoe might suggest a policeman. The audience should watch carefully as the actor transforms into the new character.

There are two levels of gameplay:

The easy version:
The actors should find two matching shoes and fully inhabit that particular character.

The challenging version:
For a greater challenge (and often hilarious results), the actors select two contrasting shoes, and enjoy the results as they try to play two characters simultaneously, one on their left side and the other on their right.

Once one actor has had the opportunity to explore the space as their new character, the next actor should go up and choose a shoe. When there are two characters in the space, they should begin interacting non-verbally in character. Continue this until all players have a character.

The aim of the game

This game allows players to explore how our manner of walking not only affects posture and physicality, but also helps to define personality. It is a fun way of creating spontaneous and often bizarre characterisations, working from an external stimulus.

2 Animal instincts

A game that encourages actors to explore characters by using animal traits, instincts and mannerisms.

How to play

Place three chairs to act as a 'bus stop', the players to sit, as 'an audience' facing them. Ask for a volunteer, let's say Ben. Ben picks a slip of paper with an animal name written on it. He must now act as a human at the bus stop, but with the characteristics of the animal he chose. In this instance he was given a fox. He sidles to the bus stop, looking around suspiciously, then balances delicately on the edge of the chair.

Ask for a second volunteer; Dave volunteers and picks a bear. He moves heavily towards the bus stop, with a stooped physicality as if tired after a long day. He sits solidly on the chair, whilst Ben watches him warily.

The two actors must interact in a manner which befits their animal choices, but remembering throughout that they are not playing the animals, merely humans with the nuances of the creatures. Ben stealthily waits until Dave is looking the other way for the bus, before he cunningly picks his pocket. Dave feels this and suddenly towers above the cowering Ben, berating him from his full height and demanding his wallet back.

Reproduced with permission, extract from *'Drama Games for Devising'* by Jessica Wale (Foreword by Mike Leigh) Nick Hern Books www.nickhernbooks.co.uk

At an appropriate moment, ask for another volunteer. Georgina goes in – she has chosen a parrot, so she struts in and immediately begins chatting away inappropriately. Ben, being the person who has been in for the longest, must the find a reason to leave the scene. With Georgina chattering away, he easily finds an excuse and slinks foxily back to the audience. Continue the game, adding in new characters each round.

Once everyone has had a go, you may wish to extend the improvisation and perhaps redistribute animals for a group scene – rush hour at the station, a night at a local hotspot or a chaotic scene in an airport terminal. Encourage the actors to find a subtle balance between animalistic nuances and human traits.

The aim of the game

The aim is to use animals as a way to explore character further, either in order to develop characters within the devised piece, or to create new characters from scratch. Primarily it is a tool to explore the multiplicity of any one character – face, body, voice and attitudes.

Further ideas when devising a scene

What sorts of different stimuli can you use to start off your ideas for the scene? Well there are any number if you think about it – people you see, locations you walk or drive past, ideas from films or TV that have stuck in your mind, objects, poems or songs. Or, how about using a photograph? If you use a photograph as a stimulus, it is important how you respond to it. Asking some basic questions about the photograph will not be enough – you must probe deeper and ask some detailed questions.

Look at the photograph of the security cameras below. The basic questions you should immediately be thinking about are included in the inner box. The more probing, detailed questions surrounding it are in the outer box.

What would be the best word to describe what these cameras are doing?

Is there anything sinister about these cameras?

Why so many cameras?

Do these cameras represent anything in your mind?

What about 'Big Brother'?

Where are they?

How many cameras are there?

What are these cameras there for?

Are these cameras there for security reasons?

What kind of building are they secured to?

What happened before these were put here?

Who are they watching?

What happened afterwards?

Activities

Make sure you understand the idea behind the questions and the inner/outer boxes.

1 Practise using the photo and box techniques with the examples of photos that follow. As you do so, try and get into the habit of asking simple and then more complex questions.

2 In a group of four or five, devise your scene based on any of the photographs of your choice. Explain your choice of photo as stimulus.

How do I use dramatic devices?

A dramatic device is any 'trick' used by playwrights to add interest to their work or create a particular impression or effect on the audience. The devices listed below are your 'toolbox' to make your scene interesting.

FREEZE-FRAME
A vivid, motionless scene or image

DRAMATIC PAUSE
During the dialogue a short silence is created – this can help to build up the tension

MIME
A storyline is acted out through movement and gesture without the character speaking

SLOW MOTION
Sometimes scenes showing events such as fights or races are shown in slow motion for greater visual effect

CROSS-CUTTING
Cross-cutting is what you do after you've created a series of scenes or sequences, and you reorder them to create a drama that goes forwards and backwards in time

THOUGHT TRACKING
A group makes a still image and individuals are invited to speak their thoughts or feelings aloud - just a few words. This can be done by tapping each person on the shoulder or holding a cardboard 'thought-bubble' above their head. Alternatively, thought tracking can involve other members of the class speaking one character's thoughts aloud for them

MONOLOGUE
A speech made by one actor in a play, film, etc., especially when alone

SYMBOLS
Dramas are produced to a great extent through the use of symbols - or representations - standing in for real things

Devised Scene

CHORAL SPEAKING
Recitation of poetry or prose by a chorus

FLASHBACKS
A transition to an earlier event or scene that interrupts the normal chronological development of the story

NARRATOR
A person who tells a story or gives an account of something

MULTI-ROLES
Actors commonly perform more than one character in a drama

DIRECT ADDRESS
An actor speaking directly to the audience

TIP
You don't have to use all the above devices in one scene. You can 'pick'n mix'!

Some examples of dramatic devices

CHORAL SPEAKING

The Chorus in the form of that school photograph of a grammar school form of fourteen/fifteen-year-old pupils all girls, circa 1962…among them are Barbara and Bernadette as well as the chorus – made up of as many girls as the director wishes, but the minimum number is nine.

The girls of the Chorus begin to recite by rote.

Chorus

I remember, I remember the house where I was born, they said. So we thought. Thing is we came from very different families.

Extract from 'Cuba' by Liz Lochhead

DIRECT ADDRESS

The narrator is an undisguised convention of the play. He takes whatever licence with dramatic convention is convenient to his purposes.

Tom enters, dressed as a merchant sailor, and strolls across to the fire escape. There he stops and lights a cigarette. He addresses the audience.

Tom

Yes I have tricks in my pocket, I have things up my sleeve. But I am the opposite of a stage magician. He gives you illusion that has the appearance of truth. I give you truth in the pleasant disguise of illusion…

Extract from 'The Glass Menagerie' by Tennessee Williams

NARRATOR

The overture comes to a close.

Mrs Johnstone (*singing*) Tell me it's not true. Say it's just a story.

The narrator steps forward

Narrator
(*speaking*)

So did y' hear the story of the Johnstone twins?
As like each other as two new pins,
Of one womb born. In the selfsame day,
How one was kept and one given away?
A' did you never hear how the Johnstones died,
Never knowing that they shared one name,
Till the day they died, when a mother cried
My own dear sons lie slain?

The lights come up to show a re-enactment of the final moments of the play – the deaths of Mickey and Edward. The scene fades.

Extract from 'Blood Brothers' By Willy Russell

CROSS-CUTTING

A hospital room. There is one bed, a bedside locker and a chair. Beyond the bed is an empty area...

DR RUTH KOVACKS enters. She comes into the empty area. In one hand she holds a sheaf of disorganised notes which she is trying to read...begins to speak to the audience.

DR KOVACKS: Sorry (*She sorts through the notes. A sudden thought*) What do you call magistrates? Are they 'Your worships'? (*Slightly apologetically*) I've never done anything like this before. I assume they just ask questions. Do they? Like in court. Well, obviously. It is a court. But do they expect... (*Still trying to get the notes in some sort of order*) Oh God... this is all out of order now...hang on. Hang on. (*A statement of her intention*) I will do this. (*Assuming some authority*) Your worships, I have been treating Miss Effie Palmer for the last three weeks...

At the sound of her name, EFFIE looks up and answers obediently but dully as if answering a register

EFFIE: Yes, Miss

DR KOVACKS (*turning to speak to her about this 'Yes Miss' business*) Effie!

Extract from 'Effie's Burning' by Valerie Windsor

MONOLOGUE

Emily: Oh, Mama, look at me one minute as though you really saw me. Mama, fourteen years have gone by. I'm dead. You're a grandmother, Mama! Wally's dead, too. His appendix burst on a camping trip to North Conway. We felt just terrible about it – don't you remember? But, just for a moment now we're all together. Mama, just for a moment we're happy. Let's really look at one another! ...I can't. I can't go on. It goes so fast. We don't have time to look at one another. I didn't realise. So all that was going on and we never noticed. Take me back – up the hill – to my grave. But first: Wait! One more look. Good-bye, Good-bye world. Good-bye, Grover's Corners....Mama and Papa. Good-bye to clocks ticking ... and Mama's sunflowers. And food and coffee. And new ironed dresses and hot baths ... and sleeping and waking up. Oh, earth, you are too wonderful for anybody to realise you. Do any human beings ever realise life while they live it – every, every minute?

Stage Manager: No. (*pause*) The saints and poets, maybe they do some.

Emily: I'm ready to go back.

Extract from 'Our Town' by Thornton Wilder

Arthur Miller readily switches from location to location during *Death of a Salesman*, as the flashback to Willy at home switches to a flashback of Willy in a hotel room in Boston.

FLASHBACK

Music is heard as behind a scrim, to the left of the house. The Woman, dimly seen, is dressing.

WILLY, *with great feeling*: You're the best there is, Linda, you're a pal, you know that? On the road – on the road I want to grab you sometimes and just kiss the life outa you.

The laughter is loud now, and he moves into a brightening area at the left, where The Woman has come from behind the scrim and is standing, putting on her hat, looking into a 'mirror' and laughing.

WILLY 'Cause I get so lonely – especially when business is bad and there's nobody to talk to. I get the feeling that I'll never sell anything again, that I won't make a living for you, or a business, a business for the boys. *He talks through The Woman's subsiding laughter! The Woman primps at the 'mirror'.* There's so much I want to make for…

THE WOMAN Me? You didn't make me, Willy. I picked you.

WILLY, *pleased* You picked me?

THE WOMAN, *who is quite proper looking, Willy's age*; I did, I've been sitting at that desk watching all the salesmen go by, day in, day out. But you've got such a sense of humour, and we do have such a good time together, don't we?

WILLY Sure, sure. *He takes her in his arms…*

John Malkovich and Dustin Hoffman in the 1985 film version of Death of a Salesman.

Devising your own scenes using dramatic devices

Activity

In groups of four or five devise your own scene using the following scenarios. Make sure you include at least three of the dramatic devices referred to on page 10. You can 'pick 'n' mix'!

SCENARIO 1

In your group start by **brainstorming** the word 'fame'. What comes to mind when you hear the word? You could create still images to show different aspects of the word.

In a group of friends there is one of them (boy or girl) who has won a local talent competition and is aiming higher by competing in a national 'X-factor' type of competition.

What tensions does this create amongst the group of friends? What relationships are there in the group? Is there a boyfriend/girlfriend? What about the family – mother/father/brother or sister – and how do they respond to the aspirations of the boy/girl in question?

Are there any jealousies? What will the outcome be?

SCENARIO 2

A young soldier seriously wounded in Afghanistan has returned home to his family and friends. They are all praying for his full recovery.

How does he respond to the concerns of his family and friends? How does he cope with his injuries? Is there a girlfriend waiting for him? How does she respond to her wounded boyfriend?

Does the young soldier have nightmares?

What about the family? What are their thoughts about the war in Afghanistan? Does the father or mother comment on war in general?

Would this be a good opportunity to use a narrator figure perhaps?

SCENARIO 3

Brian is a new boy in school. He is rather shy. The school bully has it in for him.

How do other pupils respond to the bullying of Brian? What about the teachers' reaction?

Are the parents of Brian involved? How does Brian cope? Does he have some form of escape? An escape into a world of dreams possibly.

Does the school bully learn his lesson? Do the other pupils turn against him? What about peer pressure? Don't forget that the pupil or the bully can be either a girl or a boy...

How do I structure my devised scenes?

It is important when devising your dramatic scene that you are aware of its structure. Within one scene you can include a number of dramatic highlights.

Look at the graph below and imagine that it charts a ten-minute piece of dramatic theatre.

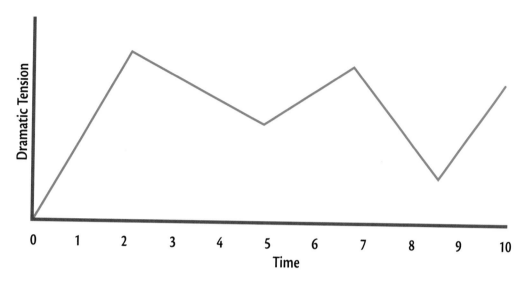

The first major highlight occurs after the first two minutes – this might be someone screaming or acting in a very aggressive manner. After this dramatic highlight the next few minutes are calmer but after the fifth minute tension begins to build up again. We reach another highlight between six and seven minutes into the piece. Tension then falls off sharply after this highlight before building up again to the final climax at the end.

This kind of graph applies to many of our modern plays. The structure of many of our plays was once compared with a bar of Toblerone.

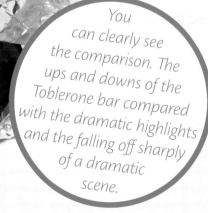

You can clearly see the comparison. The ups and downs of the Toblerone bar compared with the dramatic highlights and the falling off sharply of a dramatic scene.

Some commentators argue that if these dramatic highlights occur at the beginning or end only then the piece loses its dramatic tension. It is possible that in the middle the audience can easily lose interest. But remember that this kind of graph does not relate to *all* plays. The structure of *Macbeth* by Shakespeare, for example, can be depicted by this graph:

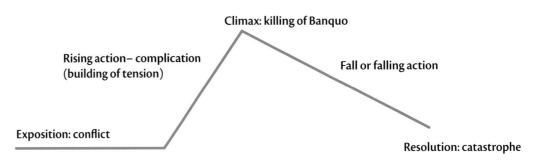

Climax: killing of Banquo

Rising action– complication (building of tension)

Fall or falling action

Exposition: conflict

Resolution: catastrophe

KEY TERMS

Exposition – makes audiences aware of the plot.

Denouement – final resolution in a play.

This structure complies with the ideas of the German playwright Gustav Freytag, who argued that a play consists of five basic parts:

Exposition (which makes audiences aware of the plot).

Rising action (in which the conflict in the play escalates to a climax).

Climax (in which the action comes to a turning point).

Falling action (in which a final twist is added to the climax).

Denouement (in which the climax is resolved and the play is brought to a conclusion).

Whatever structure you choose to follow it is always worth asking these questions when devising your scene:

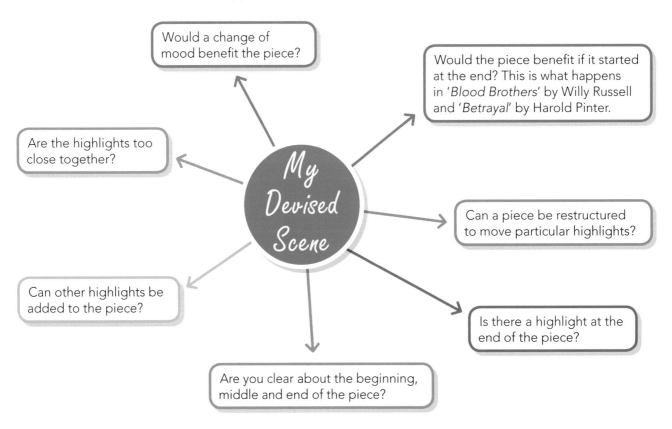

Would a change of mood benefit the piece?

Would the piece benefit if it started at the end? This is what happens in 'Blood Brothers' by Willy Russell and 'Betrayal' by Harold Pinter.

Are the highlights too close together?

My Devised Scene

Can a piece be restructured to move particular highlights?

Can other highlights be added to the piece?

Is there a highlight at the end of the piece?

Are you clear about the beginning, middle and end of the piece?

1 In groups of four or five devise a scene that responds to the news report below. Think about the following when considering your response

News

JOYRIDER, 16, AND TWO OF HIS FRIENDS KILLED IN HORROR CRASH THAT TORE CAR IN TWO

Three teenage joyriders died yesterday after their car careered off the road and slammed into a tree.

Police say the Honda Civic, which split in half on impact, was being driven by a 16-year-old.

Last night, the teenagers were named as Michael Gallagher, 16, Tom Hughes, 15, and Antonia Browne, who was due to celebrate her 15th birthday next week.

Decide on the structure of your scene.

Do you start at the end?

What leads up to the joyriding?

What is the relationship between the three friends?

Who was the **protagonist** (the main character)?

Are members of the families involved?

Will you use a narrator?

What about the involvement of the police?

How many dramatic highlights will you include?

What about the device of **thought tracking**?

Is there a one main climax in your scene?

Do you include **flashbacks** in your scene?

2 After you have completed your devised scene, draw a graph like the ones earlier in this chapter to show its dramatic structure.

KEY TERMS

Thought tracking – where someone else speaks a character's thoughts aloud for them.

Flashback – a transition to an earlier event in a series of scenes.

Creating believable characters

When you come to consider the characters in your devised scene you must remember that they can be divided into the protagonist, the antagonist and a number of other minor characters.

It must be pointed out that the antagonist can be anything, from a villain – which the hero has to overcome – to some natural disaster from which the hero is expected to save the entire world.

Can a protagonist and antagonist be the same person? Yes, that is possible but showing conflict between the two can be a challenging task. The novel 'The Strange Case of Dr Jekyll and Mr Hyde' by Robert Louis Stevenson is one of the best examples of this.

Therefore within one scene there can be major and minor characters. How do you create your own character making sure that he or she has credibility and interest for the audience?

There are a number of questions you can ask and answer in order to avoid creating a shallow character, and one way of showing you them is the Gingerbread Man. Use this tool to build up a well-rounded and comprehensive character whenever you can.

TOP TIP!

In order to get to know your character better use the technique called hot seating. This is a widely used and very effective drama strategy. Basically one person sits apart from the group in the 'hot seat' and is asked questions by other members of the group – all answers have to be in the character that's been chosen.

What is my name?

How old am I?

How do I speak?

Where do I live?

What photos or artwork are like my character, or have aspects of my character?

What are my likes?

What objects or items represent my character?

What are my dislikes?

What about my relationships with others – family, friends?

What are my hopes?

Do I have a particular status in relation to other characters?

What makes me happy?

What do I want? What is my motive?

Am I afraid of anything?

What was the worst/best moment of my life?

What is my favourite colour?

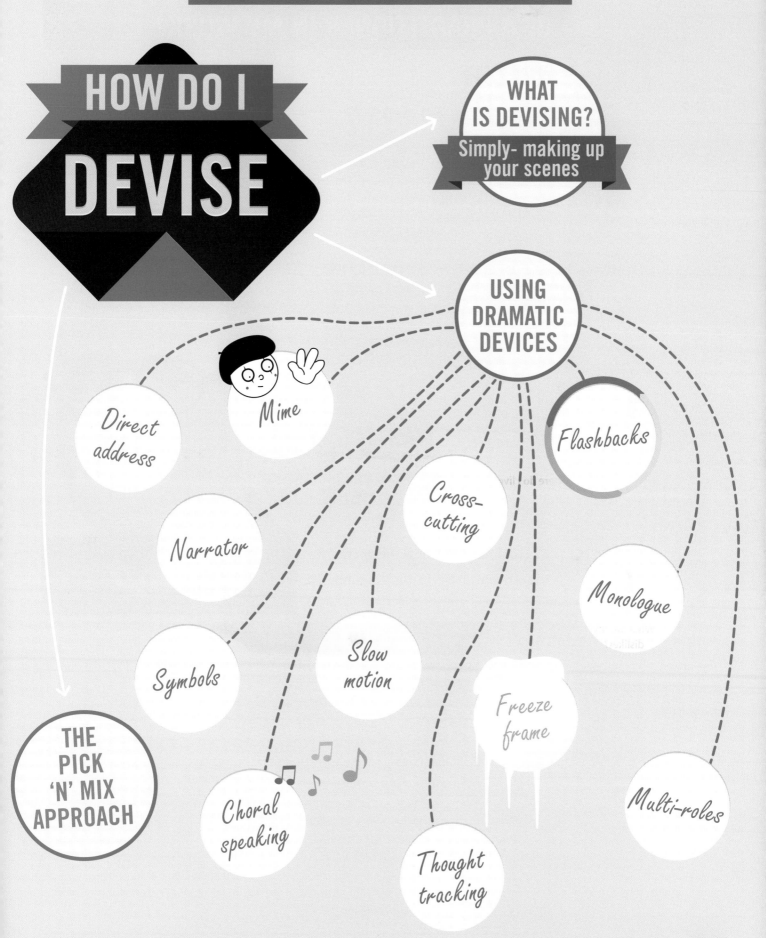

HOW DO I DEVISE

WHAT IS DEVISING?
Simply- making up your scenes

USING DRAMATIC DEVICES

THE PICK 'N' MIX APPROACH

Direct address

Mime

Narrator

Cross-cutting

Flashbacks

Symbols

Slow motion

Monologue

Choral speaking

Freeze frame

Multi-roles

Thought tracking

HOW DO I INCORPORATE THE INFLUENCES OF A PRACTITIONER IN MY WORK?

WHAT WILL I LEARN?

● You will learn about three different practitioners, their ideas for the theatre and some of the techniques they used

● How to incorporate the practitioner's ideas into your own devised scenes

KEY TERMS

Playwright – one who writes plays; a dramatist.

Practitioner – one who practices a technique.

Director – a person who supervises the creative aspects of a dramatic production and instructs the actors and crew.

Marxist ideas – according to Karl Marx (1818–83) the people of the world are divided into two groups or classes, the working class (i.e. the workers) and the ruling class (i.e. owners of factories, land and buildings). His vision was to see a classless society, where everybody is equal.

BRECHT

Who was Brecht?

Bertolt Brecht was born in Augsburg, Germany on 19 February 1898. He was a famous **playwright**, theatre critic, **practitioner** and **director**. He became one of the most influential figures in twentieth-century theatre, writing 39 plays. The first one – *Baal* – was written in 1918. His company – the *Berliner Ensemble* – became one of the most famous touring companies in the world, and to this day continues to produce politically minded work in the Brechtian style.

Some of his most well-known plays are:

● *Mother Courage and Her Children*
● *The Caucasian Chalk Circle*
● *The Threepenny Opera*
● *The Good Person of Szechwan*

FACT BRECHT was heavily influenced by Marxist ideas and he saw theatre as a way to spread political messages about class struggle.

What was his style?

You can sum up Brecht's style in **three** words:

1 **Alienation:** Brecht would use techniques which would create distance or alienation between the actor and the spectator, so that his audience would be able to respond to the drama objectively and learn from it.

2 **Didactic:** This means that he wanted his plays to have an educational purpose. They are designed to educate the performers and audience.

3 **Gestic:** This is a theatrical technique that helps define the emotion within a character and the context they are in. It is the combination of a gesture, facial expressions, body language and a social meaning into one movement, stance or vocal display. It is sometimes referred to as the 'social gest', as it is an action that allows the audience to understand something specific about the social circumstances presented on stage.

What were his ideas for the theatre?

- He wanted to distance his audience from the action, to stop them becoming too emotionally involved with the characters. His plays are often referred to as **Epic theatre**.

- He wanted to disrupt the notion of the **fourth wall**. 'Breaking the fourth wall' involves the characters directly addressing and acknowledging the audience.

- He wanted his audiences to 'think'. He wanted his theatre to show audiences that they should take the position of spectators and learn lessons from it. His plays are **didactic** because they serve to teach the audience or send messages about certain aspects of society, politics or economy.

KEY TERMS

Epic theatre – dramatic form intended to provoke rational thought rather than to create illusion.

Fourth wall – the imaginary wall between the audience and the world of the actor.

Didactic – containing a political or moral message.

DIRECT ADDRESS
An actor speaking directly to the audience

NARRATION
Where parts of the play are narrated rather than acting them telling the audience what is going on

MULTI-ROLING
Actors commonly perform more than one character in a drama

ENSEMBLE
Actors on stage at all times and who perform together

GESTUS
The combination of gesture and facial expression and body language is used to create meaning and communicate a message to the audience

SPEAKING STAGE DIRECTIONS
The actors speak the stage directions loudly directly to the audience

MUSIC/SONG
Characters frequently and suddenly burst into song – sometimes directly to the audience

PLACARDS
Signs, placards or projections which tell us what's going to happen before each scene

TICKLE AND SLAP
Lull the audience into a false sense of security and then hit them with something shocking

What techniques did Brecht use?

Examples of Brecht's techniques

The Silent Scream from the play '*Mother Courage*' is a good example of 'gestus'. The actress in this picture was Helena Vegal and she silently screamed for about two minutes. She looks at the audience and delivers this silent scream. It is not the action alone that makes it gestus, but rather the combination of this action and the social meaning. Mother Courage has just lost her son, but if she makes any sound of recognition towards him she will put her life and the life of her daughter in danger. Now she represents any person who has had to keep quiet to save somebody else. She has been forced into a terrible situation and the audience gets to see this through her gestus of a silent scream.

In this extract from '*The Caucasian Chalk Circle*' the Singer takes on the role of narrator. Her song breaks up the action as she tells the audience what is going on. This helps to keep the audience's attention and reminds them that they are watching a piece of theatre.

The Adjutant joins the procession while the rider enters the palace gateway, cursing. A soldier appears from the palace and remains standing in the gateway.

THE SINGER   The city lies still.

On the church square the pigeons preen themselves.

A soldier of the palace guard

Is jesting with the kitchen maid

As she comes up from the river with a bundle.

A girl tries to pass through the gateway, a bundle of large green leaves under her arm.

This scene is from a production of 'Mother Courage and her Children' by Brecht in a translation by Tony Kushner. It was presented at the Olivier Theatre, National Theatre, London in 2009. The image shows the use of two large 'screens' served as high-tech Brechtian placards.

KEY TERM

Reported speech – the report of one actor on the words said or thought by someone else.

More examples of Brechtian techniques

Brecht made actors turn their lines into third person narrative. Actions given in stage directions are narrated:

'Then X entered. After a few silent compliments he sat down on the sofa.'

Dialogue when spoken in a performance in the present tense, becomes **reported speech**. For example:

'Has your excellency seen the new dancing master?' becomes:

'He asked whether Madame had seen the new dancing-master.'

Brecht would include, in the text spoken in rehearsal, all stage directions. He went so far as to write what he called 'practice scenes'.

This shows how Brecht made use of speaking the stage directions during the rehearsal period.

In this extract from the play 'He Who Says Yes' by Brecht, we see once again the actor who portrays The Teacher directly addressing the audience relating who he is and what he is about to do.

```
THE TEACHER   I am the teacher. I keep a school in the city and I have a
              pupil whose father is dead; he has only his mother to look
              after him. Now I will go and say goodbye to them, for I shall
              soon be starting on a journey to the mountains. A terrible
              disease has broken out among us, and in the city beyond the
              mountains live several great doctors.

(He knocks at the door) May I come in?
```

We mustn't forget some of his more technical techniques

STAGE
Bare stage. All workings could be seen and any changes to scenery are made in full view of the audience. Using fragments of scenery and single pieces of furniture to suggest whole locations.

Technical techniques

COSTUMES
Often a single item of clothing or prop was all that was used. An actor would frequently change character or costume in front of the audience reinforcing the idea of alienation.

LIGHTING
The stage was flooded with bright white light the entire time regardless of whether the scene was summer day or winter evening.

Getting to grips with Brecht!

This series of exercises should help you further understand some of Brecht's ideas, as he is quite a challenging practitioner to get to grips with.

In one of his essays Brecht refers to a street scene, for example a re-enactment of an accident, as the basic model for epic theatre.

Activity

This exercise can be done with an individual for the whole class, or pairs for the whole class, or in small groups for each other.

There has been a road accident and as a passer-by you have been a spectator to it.

1 Imagine you are telling the story to a group of people who did not see the accident. Tell the story and include all the characters that were in it.

2 Feel free to impersonate or even caricature them.

3 Try to use gestures, narration, dialogue, third person, descriptions and even token costume and props to bring the story to life.

Brecht said that the actor, in describing the accident, must do what the witness does – SHOW or DEMONSTRATE how the accident occurred.

'The point is that the demonstrator (actor) acts the behaviour of the driver or victim or both in such a way that the bystanders are able to form an opinion of the accident.'

(Brecht)

Brecht was a massive fan of the silent film star Charlie Chaplin. He admired the control and the attention to detail in his gestural cinema performances. It's no surprise therefore that Brecht became famous for a particular style of acting called GESTUS (refer to page 21). The combination of gesture and facial expression and body language is deliberately used to create meaning and communicate a message to the audience.

Charlie Chaplin (1889–1977) was an English actor and film-maker who achieved worldwide fame for his silent movies in the early years of the 20th century. His films combined slapstick comedy with pathos, and contained social and political themes.

Activity

1 Stand in pairs at opposite sides of the room.

2 Shout nursery rhymes across the room to each other – all at the same time!

3 Can you really hear? NO! Now you have to rely on the body/gesture to get across the rhyme itself. Watch how your movements become bigger.

4 Now it is a matter of life and death importance that the rhyme is communicated. Repeat the exercise and examine use of gesture – how does it convey the importance of the message?

5 What did you do to help convey the meaning when words were limited?

Activity

In small groups create contrasting gestic depictions that demonstrate the differences in the following:

● School photo last day of term

● School photo just before an important exam

● Crowd at a football match after your team has just scored a goal

● Crowd at a football match after your team has just lost.

At all times Brecht was attempting to distance his actors from their parts, so they wouldn't become too involved. For this reason he used certain rehearsal techniques where he had his actors perform the same scene in many different ways.

To help you understand try this first activity.

Activity

1 In pairs improvise a scene in which two people (who have not seen each other for ten years) meet at a bus stop. Each actor narrates or reports exactly what they themselves are doing, and puts 'he /she said' before they speak. For instance:

```
Actor: (to the audience) 'He sat on the ground' (the actor
sits)

or

Actor: (to the audience) 'He said "It's good to see you"
(turning to actor 2) It's good to see you.'
```

a When ready, introduce thoughts aloud. These thoughts might be in contradiction to the dialogue. For instance:

> **Actor**: *(pointing at actor 2)* 'He hated the sight of him *(turning to actor 2)* How good to see you!'

b Try to use **body language** and freeze frames to suggest character and status.

Objective: to make the actor and audience view the character from a critical distance.

Activity

2 Now read this extract from *Mother Courage and her Children* and follow the instructions below:

A PEASANT *brought in by the chaplain*: My arm's gone.

THE CHAPLAIN: Where's that linen?

MOTHER COURAGE: I can't give nowt. What with expenses, taxes, loan interest and bribes. *Making guttural noises, Kattrin raises a plank and threatens her mother with it.* You gone plain crazy? Put that plank away or I'll paste you one, you cow. I'm giving nowt, don't want to, got to think of meself. *The Chaplain lifts her off the steps and sets her on the ground, then starts pulling out shirts and tearing them into strips.* My officers' shirts! Half a florin apiece! I'm ruined. *From the house comes the cry of a child in pain.*

THE PEASANT: The baby's in there still. *Kattrin dashes in.*

THE CHAPLAIN *to the woman*: Don't move. They'll get it out.

MOTHER COURAGE: Stop her, roof may fall in.

THE CHAPLAIN: I'm not going back in there.

MOTHER COURAGE *torn both ways* Don't waste my precious linen.

Kattrin brings a baby out of the ruins.

a. Read and perform the script naturalistically.

b. Read and perform the script in the third person.

c. Read and perform the script – and read the stage directions.

d. Read and perform the script explaining what you are doing as the character.

e. Return to the original script and stage the scene naturalistically again, but this time after delivering/performing each line, walk to the front of the stage and tell the audience WHY the character did/said what they did.

Activity

3 In groups of four or five devise your own scene using some of my techniques. You could choose four or five of them, e.g. narrator, direct address, multi-roling, placards, music/song. Remember that you want your audience to <u>know</u> which one they are.

Exercise

Now try using Brechtian techniques with the following stimuli:

1. *'I hope you can find it in your hearts to forgive me.'*

Discuss as a group what could have happened to make this person ask for forgiveness. Decide which one of the group will be the narrator.

The narrator can inform the audience what is going to happen.

Use placards to introduce different parts within your scene.

Take on different roles.

Use a song or music.

Remember gestures and why they are important.

When performing, you can enter the performance space as 'actors', having your costumes hanging on the stage, even doing a warm-up in front of your audience, etc.

As a group, discuss what you think this picture conveys. Look **carefully** at the characters in the picture and create your own story.

Decide which one of the group will be the narrator – the narrator can inform the audience what is going to happen.

Use placards to introduce different parts within your scene.

Take on different roles.

Use a song or music.

Remember gestures.

When performing, you can enter the performance space as 'actors' by having your costumes hanging on the stage, even doing a warm-up in front of your audience, etc.

Exercise

2. Visual stimulus

Exercise

3. What has happened?

```
The industrialist is having his aeroplane serviced.
The priest is wondering what he said about tithes in
his sermon eight weeks ago.
The generals are putting on civvies and looking like
bank clerks.
Public officials are getting friendly.
The policeman points out the way to the man in the
cloth cap.
The landlord comes to see whether the water supply
is working.
The journalists write the word People with capital
letters.
The singers sing at the opera for nothing.
Ships' captains check the food in the crew's galley,
Car owners get in beside their chauffeurs.
Doctors sue the insurance companies.
Scholars show their discoveries and hide their
decorations.
Farmers deliver potatoes to the barracks.
The revolution has won its first battle:
That's what has happened.
```

                                                    Bertolt Brecht (1898–1956)

Discuss as a group what political message is conveyed in this poem by Brecht. Decide on the structure of your scene. How will you convey the different ideas presented by Brecht?

Decide which one of the group will be the narrator. The narrator can inform the audience what is going to happen.

Use placards to introduce different parts within your scene.

Take on different roles.

Use a song or music.

Remember gestures and why they are important.

When performing, you can enter the performance space as 'actors', having your costumes hanging on the stage, even doing a warm-up in front of your audience, etc.

BRECHT

WHO WAS BRECHT?

A theatre practitioner from Germany

BRECHT'S STYLE

Alienation
Didactic
Gestic

BRECHT'S IDEAS FOR THE THEATRE

Epic theatre
No fourth wall
Didactic plays

BRECHT'S TECHNIQUES

Direct address
Narrator
Multi-roling
Ensemble
Gestus
Speaking stage directions
Music & songs
Placards
Tickle & slap

PLUS!!

Episodic structure
Political message

If I want to show Brecht's influence on my devised piece I would:

Devise a scene with an episodic structure.

Pick 'n mix from his techniques, e.g. direct address, multi-roling, narration, ensemble work, gestus, music/song and use of placards.

STANISLAVSKI

Who was Stanislavski?

Constatin Stanislavski was born in Moscow, Russia in 1863. He was a director and actor and is often referred to as the father of modern theatre. It is said that Stanislavski had a more profound effect on the process of acting than anyone else in the twentieth century.

In the late 19th century Stanislavski found the theatres styles of his day fairly dull to watch. Actors simply spoke to the audience, and did not interact very well with each other. They simply walked on stage and delivered their lines, and no effort was made to make the performances realistic. Sets were simple and unchanging, while costumes were whatever people could find or bring.

Stanislavski believed that this was not a good approach to performing. Instead of acting mechanically (with no feeling) he believed that actors should feel the emotion of the play and express it to the audience. He worked towards bettering the actor's own skill, rather than him or her just using shallow acting techniques. In order to do this he created what is referred to as the 'system', which we will look at and understand in more detail over the following pages.

> **F
> A
> C
> T**
>
> He co-founded the Moscow Art Theatre in 1897.
> Three of his most famous and important works are:
> 'An Actor Prepares'
> 'Building a Character'
> 'Creating a Role'.

Constantin Stanislavski: (1863–1938)

" WHEN YOU PLAY A GOOD MAN, TRY TO FIND OUT WHERE HE IS BAD, AND WHEN YOU PLAY A VILLAIN, TRY TO FIND WHERE HE IS GOOD. "

What were his ideas for the theatre?

Stanislavski viewed theatre as a means of artistically expressing things, and that the audience's role was to 'look in' on the action on the stage. He favoured the idea of the 'fourth wall', which separated the audience and the actors, to re-create total realism on the stage. This 'fourth wall' was an imaginary wall between the actor and the audience designed to keep the actor's attention on the stage.

It was a common practice during his time for the stars of a play to make their entrance and head straight to the front of the stage. There they took a number of bows, while the supporting cast froze in mid-action. Having received their adulation, the stars would return to the drama of the play, at which point the supporting cast unfroze and the performance would continue.

Stanislavski wanted to get away from this star system, and away from the habit of the time that the actors play to the audience rather than to each other. He felt that a new approach to theatre would move it away from one which – in his opinion – lacked artistic integrity and inner substance. He wanted the audience to feel the pain or joy of the actor, and that watching a performance would bring out a feeling of empathy in the person in the audience.

Stanislavski believed in ensemble acting and wanted to take theatre away from the idea of having a star who was the most important in the show. His belief was to create something as near to naturalism as possible.

What is Stanislavski's 'system'?

The system is sometimes referred to as 'the method'.
- The 'system' is a set of rules and exercises which create a foundation from which actors are able to work.
- Stanislavski's 'system' uses internal and external techniques to gain a full analysis of the character and how they should be portrayed.
- The **internal** techniques refer to the creation of the character: emotions, inner-feelings, desires and impulses.
- The **external** techniques refer to the actor becoming the role: physical movement, facial expressions, words, mannerisms and voice.

CONCENTRATION OF ATTENTION

RELAXATION OF MUSCLES

FEELING OF TRUTH

Internal techniques

UNITS AND OBJECTIVES

THE MAGIC 'IF'

EMOTION MEMORY

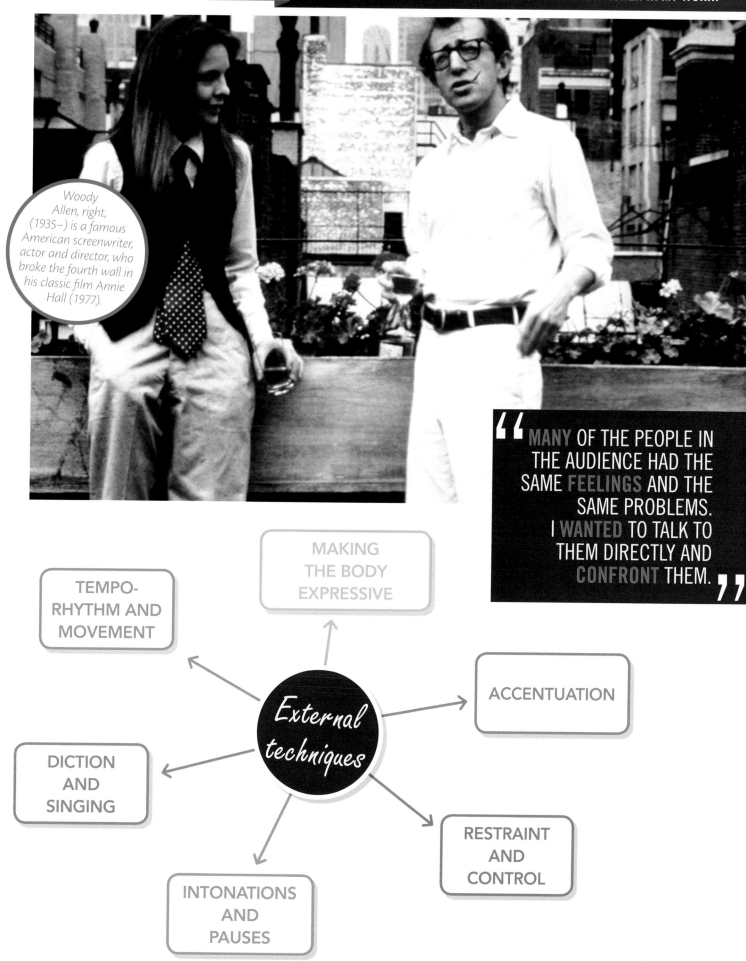

Woody Allen, right, (1935–) is a famous American screenwriter, actor and director, who broke the fourth wall in his classic film Annie Hall (1977).

" MANY OF THE PEOPLE IN THE AUDIENCE HAD THE SAME FEELINGS AND THE SAME PROBLEMS. I WANTED TO TALK TO THEM DIRECTLY AND CONFRONT THEM. "

MAKING THE BODY EXPRESSIVE

TEMPO-RHYTHM AND MOVEMENT

ACCENTUATION

External techniques

DICTION AND SINGING

RESTRAINT AND CONTROL

INTONATIONS AND PAUSES

Internal techniques in detail

Relaxation of muscles

Stanislavski believed that muscular tension did not help the actor when they tried to enter into the feelings of the part. If the actor was in a relaxed state of mind then they could focus and concentrate upon the play fully. This is why Stanislavski placed relaxation at the foundation of his 'system'.

Ideas for relaxation exercises:

1 Lay on the floor with your eyes closed and imagine you are lying on a beach, slowly sinking into the sand. Allow your muscles to sink into the floor, your tension draining away. Tense each of your lower leg muscles, then relax. Work your way up your body tensing and relaxing the different muscles. Notice the difference in your overall relaxation before and after the exercise.

2 'Rag doll': an exercise in total relaxation. Imagine you are a rag doll, hanging from nails. Someone picks you up and throws you down to the floor. How does your body react to this?

3 Imagine a wooden fence, the bottom of which is quite low to the ground – say about 40 cm or so. First crawl under the imaginary fence, gradually pushing your head and shoulders under it. The when you are all the way through, crawl back under the fence but this time go through backwards.

4 Get down on all fours. First lazily roll on to your back and stretch, like a cat, and then contract. Then, arch your back, hiss and adopt a defensive position.

Concentration

This element is about concentrating on the stage and ignoring the fact that there is an audience watching. Stanislavski wanted his actors to separate themselves from the audience, and use their imagination to overcome the sensation of the audience acknowledging their existence. It is obvious that concentration was important to Stanislavski because his work is riddled with references to it.

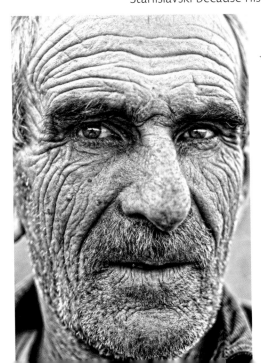

Ideas for concentration exercises:

1 You are given an object and asked to study it. You then have to describe its shape, colour, use, special features. The object is then removed and you are asked to tell the group what you remember, what caught your attention. You are then given the object again and a comparison is made between the real object and the remembered object.

2 Study a person in a picture. The picture is taken away. Describe what you saw. Compare your description with the picture. This is one example for you to start with:

Activity

Now you are asked to concentrate and pay special attention to detail:

3 Arrange a number of objects on the table – books, pencils, pens, papers, mirrors, etc. Four or five students go to the table and study the arrangement. Then, while they have their backs turned, or are out of the room, rearrange everything. On their return, they must put everything back as it was.

HINT
Remember when responding to a picture or photograph to look in more detail at what is shown – not going just for the obvious!

Activity

In this next task your concentration and paying attention to detail will lead to action:

4. In groups of four or five, look at a reproduction of a well-known painting, or a newspaper photograph. Study the people in it carefully, the way they are behaving, sitting, standing. Create the situation that led to this point. Then act out the situation.

This is one example you can start with:

Emotion memory

With emotion memory the actor remembers a situation when they felt the same – or very similar – emotions as their character. Recalling the situation leads to emotion. For Stanislavski, an effective emotion memory is the actor's 'store-room' because it is piled high with all sorts of experiences and emotions. Recalling how you felt during a certain situation in the past, and looking for the comparisons with the situation of your character, helps you to create a more believable character.

1. Choose a two-person scene. Determine the emotion in the scene. For example, envy.

2. Recall a memory from your own life where you felt envy. Write the memory down. Be specific. Try to use the five senses in your description. For example:

   'My best friend and I tried out for the same part in the school play. She got it and I didn't. I tried to be happy for her, but I wasn't. I couldn't look her in the eye. I made my voice sound happy, but I knew I was exaggerating and I think she did too. My stomach hurt and I had to hold it. I thought I was going to throw up.'

3. Devise a scene involving envy. It does not have to be the scenario of your memory. But, keep your memory in your mind. Remember how you acted.

4. Perform the scene.

The magic 'if'

Stanislavski encouraged his students to use the magic 'if' to believe in the circumstances of the play. Actors use their imagination to answer questions like:

- What would I do **if**...there were a mad axe-murderer behind the door? (This is one of Stanislavski's own examples.)
- What would I do **if** I knocked someone over in my car?
- What would I do **if** I were nominated for an Oscar?

Answering such questions makes the actor use their imagination and since Stanislavski devotes a whole chapter to imagination in his book '*An Actor Prepares*', it's obvious that he considered it to be an important tool in any actor's 'toolbox'.

A volunteer is to act as though they are walking down the street. The other students then ask... 'What if...' and make a suggestion to the volunteer to act out a situation. This may be, 'What if you were attacked by an old lady?'. It may be appropriate that the other student becomes the old lady.

The reactions to WHAT IF need to be spontaneous and need to be as realistic and naturalistic as possible. Other examples could include: 'What if you were hit by a bus?', then 'What if you fell over and had broken your leg?'

The other two internal techniques in Stanislavski's system were:

- **Feeling of truth:** the actor must believe in what they are doing. Only if the actor believes, will the audience believe.
- **Units and objectives:** units are units of action, which involves breaking each scene down, looking at the character's speech, intention and movement. The objectives are what the character wants to achieve.

External techniques in detail

Making the body expressive

Stanislavski thought that an actor's body should be physically prepared for the performance. He felt the body should be toned and agile, with stamina and flexibility. Any physical exercises carried out by the actor should make their body more expressive, because this would help them to pay particular attention to the movements, mannerisms and gestures of the character.

> **HINT**
>
> Before you try any exercises or activities using the body, why not repeat the rag-doll activity from page 32. This will help get your body relaxed.

Activity

1. To focus on agility: walk in a clockwise/anti-clockwise direction. Then touch your toes and turn round twice. Then touch your shoulders, knees and the floor in quick succession. Finish with a combination of all four moves.

2. Use your body to express the following:
   a. Writing a letter – what kind of letter is it, happy, serious, important?
   b. Packing a suitcase – where are you going, for how long, what is the climate, what kind of clothes will you need?
   c. Reading a newspaper – what will you find in the newspaper, bad or good news about one of your friends, news about a famous person, a national tragedy?
   d. Moving a heavy table from one end of the room to another.
   e. You are in a library where absolute silence is required. You and your friend are sitting in different parts of the room. Use your body to indicate very discreetly that you both have to leave because you have an appointment.

3. In pairs, choose one of the pictures below and act out the conversation that you think is going on between the two people shown BUT you can use movements, gestures, hands and facial expressions <u>only</u>. Do not use words!

Accentuation

Emphasising the incorrect word in a sentence can change the context and meaning of the whole story. Being clear of what is to be accentuated is vital.

1. Take a sentence like this one: 'What are you doing?' and say it in as many different ways as possible – emphasising different words. Each time, the sentence should convey a different meaning.

2. Take the following two sentences and again say them in as many different ways as possible:

   'Please go away. I'm waiting for someone.'

3. Look at this short dialogue from the play '*Tartuffe*' by Moliere:

```
[Valere and Mariane have quarrelled]
Valere: All right, if that's the way you want it....
Mariane: Fine!
Valere: You'll never set eyes on me again.
Mariane: Suits me!
Valere: (turning to the door) What?
Mariane: Well?
Valere: Did you say something?
Mariane: Me? You're dreaming.
Valere: Well, I'll be off then. Goodbye.
Mariane: Goodbye!
```

After reading the dialogue together, in pairs play around with it so that words start to have different emphases, or stand out suddenly. Decide how quickly you are going to speak and what particular word or line you are going to emphasise or draw attention to.

Tempo-rhythm

Tempo is how quickly or slowly something is said, or the speed of a piece of music, for instance. The varying speeds and timings of both actions and speech on stage coincide to produce a rhythm. At its most simple, 'tempo' is the speed at which you carry out an action, and 'rhythm' is the intensity with which you carry it out.

1. Thinking of the speed and intensity of your action, sit down when you are bad tempered, and then sit down again just after hearing bad news.

2. Thinking again of the speed at which you will carry out the action and the intensity with which you carry it out, create a situation around the following tasks:

   a. Looking for something you have lost.

   b. Tidying your room.

   c. As a thief, open a window, listen, enter quietly and quickly; stop to listen; open a door; go along a corridor, up the stairs and turn to listen.

   d. Hiding.

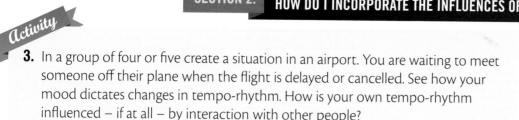

3. In a group of four or five create a situation in an airport. You are waiting to meet someone off their plane when the flight is delayed or cancelled. See how your mood dictates changes in tempo-rhythm. How is your own tempo-rhythm influenced – if at all – by interaction with other people?

The other external techniques in Stanislavski's system

- Restraint and control: an actor must avoid unnecessary gesture, and must avoid over-acting.
- Diction: Stanislavski believed that every actor must have excellent diction and pronunciation.
- Intonation and pauses: Stanislavski warns against monotone speech, unless it is in the character's portrayal. An actor must use pitch, pace and pauses to give more meaning to what the character has to say.

Perhaps the final note on the methods and ideas Stanislavski brought to theatre is that he suggested there were seven steps to building a character:

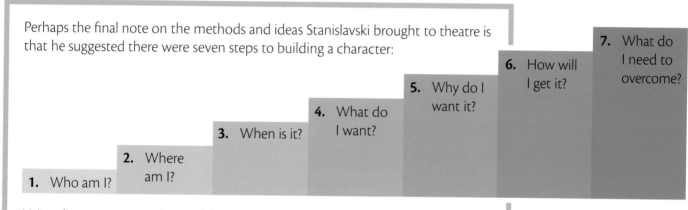

1. Who am I?
2. Where am I?
3. When is it?
4. What do I want?
5. Why do I want it?
6. How will I get it?
7. What do I need to overcome?

Using these seven questions will help you recognise the purpose of your character and your movement on stage.

Use Stanislavski's seven steps idea – and any of the other Stanislavski techniques you have learnt – to help you create your own devised scene. Do this in groups of four or five people. Use your imagination to create realistic scenes and characters based on the following stimuli:

1. Take two or three different objects and link them together to form a scenario. Select, for example, a mirror, a watch, a shirt, a bouquet of flowers, a handkerchief, a lottery ticket, an umbrella, house keys or some cash.

2. Consider the following title:

I WAS LOST!

What does that convey to you? Create a scenario based just on those words. Where were you lost? What had happened and how did you feel? Who was with you – if anyone? Who are the other characters in your story?

In the process of creating these scenes take your turn to be in the hot seat and have other members of the group or class ask you questions and you answer in character.

[Some of the exercises in this section were borrowed and adapted from '*Stanislavski and the Actor*' by Jean Benedetti (Methuen) and '*The Complete Stanislavsky Toolkit*' by Bella Merlin (Nick Hern Books)]

STANISLAVSKI

WHO WAS STANISLAVSKI?

A theatre practitioner from Russia

STANISLAVSKI'S IDEAS FOR THE THEATRE

The audience's role was to look in on the action on stage

The fourth wall — which separated the audience and the actor

STANISLAVSKI'S TECHNIQUES

INTERNAL TECHNIQUES

Feeling of truth
Relaxation of muscle
The magic 'if'
Emotion memory
Concentration of attention
Units and objectives

EXTERNAL TECHNIQUES

Making the body expressive
Accentuation
Restraint & control
Diction & singing
Intonation & pauses
Tempo-rhythm & movement

If I want to show Stanislavski's influence on my devised piece I would:

Use the technique of emotion memory — in order to create a believable character.

Use the technique of concentration on stage.

Use the 'magic if' in order to believe in the circumstances of the devised piece.

Avoid monotone speech and acquire excellent diction and pronunciation.

AUGUSTO BOAL

Who was Augusto Boal?

Augusto Boal was born in Rio de Janeiro, Brazil on 16 March 1931. He died there on 2 May 2009. He was a revolutionary Brazilian theatre director, dramatist and politician who created the Theatre of the Oppressed. This was a radical new form of **interactive theatre** intended to transform lives as the spectators become performers, acting out solutions to social problems. Boal began his career with the Arena Theatre in Sao Paulo in 1956; he was its director until 1971, and it was during this time that he developed his theories about theatre.

Brazil in the 1960s

In order to fully understand Boal's Theatre of the Oppressed you will need to know a bit about the conditions in Brazil during the 1960s. Brazil during this period was governed by a dictatorship, which meant that one person (or a group of people) ruled Brazil and had all the power and control over laws and rules. There was no government to help to make decisions – the decisions the dictator made were final.

In Britain today, we have 'freedom of speech' – anyone can (with some exceptions) express an opinion or point of view, even if that goes against what the government are doing. This was not the case in Brazil in the 1960s. The military dictatorship there would do what it wanted to do without consulting the people in the country, and would still do it even if they knew the Brazilians would not agree with it, or it would mean that they were being oppressed.

Boal was trying to help people to become free from oppression through his plays, but this was illegal. Therefore Boal continually ran the risk of being arrested or killed for speaking out against the military dictatorship. And this is what actually happened to him – he was arrested in 1971 by the military **junta** then ruling Brazil and spent the next 15 years in exile.

This photo was taken in Brazil in 1969 and shows a torture technique in which the victim was tied to a windmill-like structure called a 'resting place'

What were his ideas for the theatre?

Boal saw the theatre as a means of promoting social and political change. He wanted his theatre to stimulate people to think and act, rather than simply receive a message.

He considered that preaching to people about what they should do was arrogant, and believed that theatre should instead provide them with the means to transform their own lives and discover their own solutions.

In an effort to transform theatre from the 'monologue' of traditional performance into a 'dialogue' between audience and stage, Boal experimented with many kinds of interactive theatre. Theatre then became an extraordinary tool for transforming monologue into dialogue. 'While some people make theatre,' said Boal, 'we all are theatre'.

His techniques and theories have been applied in schools, prisons and psychiatric hospitals, as well as by theatre companies, in more than 50 countries around the world.

Boal's techniques

Forum Theatre

This is a type of theatrical game where a problem is shown in an unresolved form. The audience is invited to suggest and enact solutions. The scenario is then repeated, allowing the audience to offer alternative solutions. The game is a contest between the audience and actors trying to bring the play (or usually an issue of oppression) to a different end. The result is a pooling of knowledge, tactics and experiences. As the audience participate in enacting solutions to break the cycle of oppression they are also 'rehearsing for life'.

Boal's preferred approach to Forum Theatre is as follows:

1. The actors (either professional actors or non-professionals drawn from oppressed communities) perform a play with a scripted core. In this play, an oppression relevant to the audience is played out.
2. After reaching the scripted conclusion, in which the oppressed character(s) fail to overturn their oppression, the actors begin the production again. Usually, though, it is done in a reduced, shortened form. At any point during this second performance, any 'spect-actor' may call out 'stop!'
3. They then take the place of the actor portraying the oppressed individual. The original actor stays on stage but to one side, giving suggestions to the 'spect-actor'.
4. The 'spect-actor' then attempts to overturn the oppression using some method unused by the actors. The actors portraying the oppressors improvise to attempt to bring the production to its original, scripted ending. If the audience believes that the spect-actor's actions are too unrealistic to be utilised in reality, they may call out 'magic!', and the spect-actor must modify the actions accordingly.
5. If this spect-actor fails to overthrow the oppression, the actor resumes their character, and continues the production until another spect-actor calls out 'stop!' and attempts a different method.
6. If and when the oppression has been overthrown by the spect-actors, the production changes again: the spect-actors now have the opportunity to replace the oppressors, and find new ways of challenging the oppressed character. In this way a more realistic depiction of the oppression can be made by the audience, who are often victims of the oppression.

CASESTUDY

Cardboard Citizens is a homeless people's professional theatre company. They use Forum Theatre in their productions.

Birds is about Don, who as a young girl is persuaded to carry drugs to the Caribbean, in exchange for a holiday. She gets caught at Heathrow and is given eight years in prison. After she gets out of jail, her stepfather opposes her mother's plan to help her. Don ends up living in a squat with a man who provides her with drugs, cheats on her and gives her a sexual disease.

The actors performed the 20-minute play. Then they performed it again allowing the audience to stop the action whenever they thought Don could have taken better decisions.

Each actor had to do their best to keep things the way they were originally, unless the person who intervened was persuasive enough. A woman stood up and argued that if Don was nice to her angry stepfather he would be more understanding. She acted it out and it actually worked. Everyone burst out laughing at her extreme patience and at the man's change of attitude.

Image Theatre

This approach consists of creating short scenes each no longer than a minute or two. Each one has a strong image that the entire audience can easily understand, identify, and apply to their own lives. Participants are asked to 'mould' and 'sculpt' their own bodies or those of others into individual representations of a particular situation, emotion, or idea. They then move into a group and re-form the images they have created to form a picture or 'image'. Boal encouraged the participants to immediately create an image rather than think about it, because he felt that by thinking too much the participants would defeat the purpose of expressing raw, unrefined perceptions on an idea or issue.

Images can be realistic, allegorical, surrealistic, symbolic or metaphorical. The only thing that matters is that it is true; that it is felt as true by the protagonist. Images tell the story in a condensed, outline form using pictures with very little or no talking. The audience is pulled in immediately because they know exactly what is being said. Movement, music, and ensemble are used to heighten the impact.

Generally, this form of theatre is also used to express oppressions.

Invisible Theatre

This approach is where a previously rehearsed play is performed in a public space without the public knowing that it is a play. It addresses a precise theme concerning social injustice, such as sexism, racism or ageism. It is intended to provoke debate and to clarify the problem with the people who experience it.

The actors involved will work from a scripted core, but improvisation is utilised to get the community involved in discussing the issue being performed. Often the actors will not just consist of the oppressors and the oppressed, but also those pretending to be passers-by who voice strong (and contrasting) opinions on the subject, as a means of encouraging the 'real' passers-by to do the same.

Those practising Invisible Theatre are often seen as activists and it is not uncommon for them to come into conflict with the authorities and/or Police. Invisible Theatre's main aim is to reveal the violence that exists in society and to draw attention to recurring and common problems.

Theatre of the Oppressed

> When I saw all the oppression that existed in Brazil in the 1960s that's when I created 'Theatre of the Oppressed'.

Let's try and define the term 'oppression' and see how it links to someone's status.

What comes to the mind when you hear the word 'oppression'?

- Make a mind map of the word 'oppression'.
- How many different types of oppression can you think of?
- What feelings might people have if they are being oppressed?
- How does status link to oppression?

Activity

1a. Everyone in the group stands in a circle with their eyes closed. The teacher will walk around the circle and touch everyone on the back, but attach a sticker saying 'OPPRESSOR' to five pupils' backs – none of you will know who the oppressors are yet, because everyone has been touched on the back.

b. You then begin to move around the space and react appropriately to one another, so that you can work out whether you are oppressed or the oppressor. Once you know that you are the oppressor/oppressed, how do you move? How do you look at people? Do the oppressed stand together?

c. At the end of the activity students comment on the way they showed the difference in their status.

   This must be a silent activity – possibly with music in the background to create atmosphere.

2. In groups of four or five, consider the following news item from Brazil in the 1960s:

> Reporting from Sao Paulo, Brazil — Vera Paiva has spent four decades trying to find out what happened to her father after he was arrested in 1965 during Brazil's military dictatorship.

  a. Devise a scene based on this news item. Remember to use a variety of dramatic devices – narrator, cross-cutting, flashbacks, thought tracking, freeze frames, etc.
  b. Why was the father arrested? What happened to him?
  c. What are the thoughts of the daughter?
  d. What are the feelings of the oppressors?

An important work – Boal's '*Games for Actors and Non-Actors*'

In 1992 Boal published *Games for Actors and Non-Actors*, which describes techniques for putting his ideas into practice. It is a valuable handbook of methods, techniques, games and exercises and is designed to help anyone to make the fictional real.

These are just a few examples of his games and exercises.

1. The cross and the circle

Participants are asked to describe a circle with their right hand. Large or small, as they please. It's easy, everybody does it. Stop. Ask them to do a cross with their left hand. Even easier. Everyone gets there. Stop. Ask them to do both at the same time. It's almost impossible. In a group of thirty people, sometimes one person manages it, almost never two. Three is the record!

2. Ball games

Football, basketball, volleyball, etc. Two teams play a match without using a ball, but acting as if there was one. A referee must check to see if the imaginary movements of the ball correspond closely enough to the real movements of the actors, and should correct them if necessary. Any kind of collective sport can be played for this kind of exercise – ping-pong, tennis, etc.

3. Building character relations

This exercise can be either silent or with sound. One actor starts an action. A second approaches and, by means of visible physical gestures, establishes a relationship with him, in keeping with the nature of the role he has chosen – brother, father, son, uncle, etc. The first actor must work out what this role is and respond accordingly. Immediately after, a third person starts up a relationship with the first two, then in comes a fourth, and so on. The first part of this exercise must be silent, so that the relationships with the outside world develop via the senses and not through words.

4. Space and territory

A woman is sitting on a crowded subway. All the seats are taken except for one seat beside her, which is empty. A man boards the carriage and sits beside her – her territory has not been invaded.

The same woman is sitting in the same seat, and the whole carriage is empty. The same man comes and sits by her: her territory is invaded. In this Forum game, spect-actors replace the woman and show different ways of regaining their territory.

Extracts taken from '*Games for Actors and Non-Actors*' Augusto Boal.
Translated by Adrian Jackson. Reproduced with thanks to Routledge 2002

Over to you... Devise YOUR OWN Image Theatre!

Individually form an image of the emotion or feeling conveyed by this picture.

In groups of four or five bring your images together to represent an overall impression of the situation. Try to make your images relate to each other, by turning to face one another, moving closer, etc.

As a group, create an 'ideal image'; what would the image look like if the oppression was overthrown, i.e. the participants were not being oppressed any more.

Now the group needs to create the **transitional image**; how will they get from oppressed to ideal? What would need to happen in reality for the ideal image to become real?

KEY TERM

Transitional image – an image which moves from one feeling or emotion or situation to another.

Devise YOUR OWN Forum Theatre

Poverty is a form of oppression. In groups of four or five devise a scene about a family in poverty.

The father is out of work. There are three children to feed and clothe. They cannot face paying the rent. They are faced with homelessness.

Where will they live? A garage? In the back of a van? On wasteland in a shack they build themselves?

Where will the money to buy food come from? Is there any food left in the fridge?

What are their feelings and emotions?

Perform the scene in front of an audience (the other pupils in your class) and invite them to stop the action if they so wish and provide any answers they may have to resolve the problems facing the family. This in turn will change the nature of the scene.

Then discuss your experiences of performing this piece of Forum Theatre.

Devise YOUR OWN Invisible Theatre

In groups or four or five read the following news story, which suggests a possible example of racism for you to work from.

 News

SCHOOLGIRL ARRESTED FOR REFUSING TO STUDY WITH NON-ENGLISH PUPILS

A teenage schoolgirl was arrested by police for racism after refusing to sit with a group of Asian students because some of them did not speak English.

Codie Stott's family claim she was forced to spend three-and-a-half hours in a police cell after she was reported by her teachers.

The 14 year old – who was released without charge – said it had been a simple matter of common sense and accused the school and police of an over-the-top reaction.

The incident happened in the same local education authority where a ten-year-old boy was prosecuted earlier this year for calling a school friend racist names in the playground, a move branded by a judge 'political correctness gone mad'.

Codie was attending a GCSE Science class at Harrop Fold High School in Worsley, Greater Manchester, when the incident happened.

The teenager had not been in school the day before due to a hospital appointment and had missed the start of a project, so the teacher allocated her a group to sit with.

'She said I had to sit there with five Asian pupils', said Codie yesterday.

'Only one could speak English, so she had to tell that one what to do so she could explain in their language. Then she sat me with them and said "Discuss".'

According to Codie, the five – four boys and a girl – then began talking in a language she didn't understand, thought to be Urdu, so she went to speak to the teacher.

'I said "I'm not being funny, but can I change groups because I can't understand them?" But she started shouting and screaming, saying "It's racist, you're going to get done by the police".'

Devise a scene based on this news story. Remember to use a variety of dramatic devices. Remember your 'toolbox'!

If it is practical, try to perform your scene outside the drama studio or your school hall. For example, could you perform it in a local cafe, the local library, or just on the street?

If possible get the response of the audience around you to the action, and invite them to discuss the situation.

BOAL

WHO WAS AUGUSTO BOAL?
A theatre practitioner from Brazil

BOAL'S IDEAS FOR THE THEATRE
Promoting social political change

Interactive Theatre

BOAL'S TECHNIQUES
Forum Theatre
Image Theatre
Invisible Theatre
Theatre of the Oppressed

Audience invited to enact and suggest solutions to the issues in the play

Creating short scenes with strong images that the audience can easily understand

A rehearsed play performed in a public place

Acting out a situation which shows oppression and how it can be overcome

If I want to show Boal's influence on my devised piece I would:

Include short scenes with a strong image that the audience can easily understand and identify with.

Include an example of oppression and show a resolution to the situation which the audience can agree or disagree with.

If possible, perform a scene dealing with an example of social injustice in a public place.

HOW DO I INCORPORATE THE INFLUENCES OF A GENRE IN MY WORK?

WHAT WILL I LEARN?

○ You will learn about three different theatre genres which will help you to incorporate some of the ideas involved into your own devised scenes.

A. THEATRE IN EDUCATION

What is Theatre in Education?

Theatre in Education (TIE) starts with an educational topic or debate and develops a show around it. It is more than simply a drama performance, because it may turn into a programme of events that can include a performance supported by active audience participation. The actors use a variety of techniques to explore certain sensitive issues that the audience are familiar with. It can also be used to bring to life history and great literature by pulling students into the story in role.

When did TIE start?

Theatre in Education started as a separate art form and educational activity in Coventry at the Belgrade Theatre in 1965. A group consisting of actors, teachers and social workers were brought together to create theatrical performances and drama workshops. Their aim was to explore issues of cultural, social, political and moral significance as part of a free service to schools and the young people of Coventry.

It was a ground-breaking project, and word soon spread to other UK theatres and beyond. To this day it is an on-going international success story, which continues to benefit millions of young people all over the world.

Belgrade Theatre Coventry

The ethos of TIE is clear in the Belgrade Theatre's belief that 'theatre can enrich communities and fundamentally change people's lives for the better.' The new theatre buildings were opened in 2007.

Examples of present day TIE companies

CragRats are an innovative Theatre-in-Education provider with a long record of changing young people's mindset through live-drama, hard hitting media and accelerated learning. With over 25 years of industry-leading expertise, CragRats has grown into one of Britain's most admired education and training companies.

Gazebo is one of the oldest TIE companies in the UK, having been set up in 1979. It continues to provide inspirational TIE programmes and arts activities for children and young people. In addition to their core education programmes – which were developed to support Every Child Matters and the National Curriculum – Gazebo works with community groups, local authorities and regional and national organisations to develop a diverse range of arts- and issue-based activities.

ARAD GOCH (from their own website) Formed in 1989, Arad Goch creates new work primarily for young audiences. The company's repertoire combines both contemporary and traditional source material with a variety of physical and imagistic theatre, contemporary and traditional performance styles and live music. The company creates new work by:

1. Commissioning new plays.

2. Adapting children's and young people's literature for the stage.

3. Devising work with regular groups of performers.

The company tours main-stage productions and small scale, studio productions.

TIP

Why not search for examples of other TIE companies, including some that are based near you.

Theatr NaNog was established in 1982 to produce theatre for a wide range of audiences throughout Wales in a variety of venues and locations in both languages. The literal translation of Theatr na nÓg is 'theatre of eternal youth' and this neatly summarises the ethos of the of the Company – it aims to create theatre that has the power to excite and engage audiences of all ages.

To help you when you devise your own TIE scenes here are some examples of previous TIE productions. The issues they have dealt with may help you with your ideas.

Pow Wow! was the name of the first known TIE project. It involved the participating children meeting a cowboy (played by an actor), then meeting an imprisoned Native American (played by another actor). The children got to hear both of their arguments and predicaments, before deciding as a group whether they should free the Indian or not. (**Belgrade Theatre Coventry**)

'**Hope**' is a contemporary and powerful production that combines music and drama. It tells the story of three young people who are all affected by bullying in different ways. The performance is followed by participatory workshops that encourage pupils to use decision-making skills and ultimately decide the outcome of the play. (**The Take Away Theatre Company**)

'**Where There's A Will, There's a Play**' is set in the year 1615 when King James was the monarch. In the courtyard of an inn somewhere in England the 11 strong touring company of 'Bishop Carey's Men' are scheduled to give a performance of William Shakespeare's 'The Merchant of Venice'. But unfortunately most of them get arrested, leaving only three: Henry, Cedric and Edmund, to entertain the gathered audience. Undeterred our intrepid heroes decide to perform extracts from Shakespeare's most popular plays: *Macbeth, Dream, Romeo and Juliet* and *The Tempest*, (with a little help from the audience when required); between which we hear about their lives under the Tudors and Stuarts. After the show the audience are invited to ask questions about Shakespeare's works and times. (**Bitesize Theatre Company**)

A Little to the Left of Centre. This play was aimed at young people aged 12 and 13 years old. The play deals with a range of issues that are currently facing young people, with a particular focus on web safety and cyber bullying. The play follows the story of a teenage boy and his transition to High School from Middle School. Tensions fray as his best friend gradually becomes a victim of bullying. The 40-minute play is followed by a post-performance workshop in which the issues raised are discussed and explored further. The play encourages young people to make their own decisions and judgements based on the scenarios that are presented to them. (**Full House Theatre Company**)

cwmni theatr arad goch

Arad Goch Theatre Company – based in Aberystwyth, Mid Wales, visited schools with their production of *'Tafliad Carreg'*. This was an adaptation of *'Stones'* by Tom Lycos and Stefo Nantsou and it tells the story of two boys, one a 15 year old and the other a 13 year old. They are brought before the court accused of killing a driver by throwing a stone at his car from a bridge overlooking a busy highway. The stimulus for the authors was a disturbing headline in a newspaper in Australia where the incident happened, *'Boys on Death Charge'.*

What are the 6 steps you should take when devising your own TIE production?

6 **Evaluation**
There should be a general class discussion on the different presentations and you should consider the audience's reaction. How did they respond to the piece, and what differences were there – if any – between the final rehearsal and the actual performance?

5 **Audience participation**
After performing your scene you must be prepared to involve the audience in your production. Prepare questions you would ask them on the chosen topic, asking them for their opinions, even giving them a chance to give an alternative ending to your scene.

4 **Writing your devised scene**
In groups of four or five structure your scene using some of the devising techniques you learned in Section 1. Remember, for example:

Narrator   *Direct address*   *Flashbacks*
Monologue   *Multi-roles*

3 **Researching your topic**
Before you start devising your scene, you must research your topic thoroughly. Use the Internet, books, newspaper articles, the local library or first-hand experiences from friends and relatives (depending on the chosen topic).

2 **Deciding on the topic of your scene**
There are so many topics you could choose from but when considering what issues you want to discuss you must consider the target audience you decided upon. Examples could include road safety, drug and alcohol abuse, health and safety, environmental, ethnic, moral, cultural and social issues, personal and family relationships, social skills, arts and cultural awareness.

1 **Deciding on your target audience**
Who is the audience: primary school pupils, Year 7 pupils, senior pupils or adults?

The following exercises will help you to explore this whole genre further, and will also give you food for thought when considering how to devise your own scene.

Exercise 1 Dilemmas

1. Consider the idea of a **dilemma** and what it means to you. In groups of four or five consider the dilemmas below.

DILEMMA 1

You are walking down the street and go past a Travel Money Exchange. You come across a bundle of cash that has been dropped. You can't see anyone, what do you do?

DILEMMA 2

You are out on the street and you get into an argument with someone, you lose your temper quickly and hit them. There are lots of people around and confusion quickly ensues. Unbeknown to you, two police officers have seen the incident and immediately come over to address the problem. They have not seen the incident clearly but they think, rightly, that you threw a punch. They immediately begin to question you and accuse you of the incident. Your best friend interferes and says that they threw the punch and that you are innocent. Do you go against your friend and confess to the crime, or do you allow them to take the blame?

DILEMMA 3

You are on a social networking site and someone you have been talking to for three months asks to meet you. Do you go?

DILEMMA 4

You think your boyfriend/girlfriend has been cheating on you and you believe that the texts that will prove this are on their phone. Do you secretly look at their phone?

DILEMMA 5

In a shop your friend suggests you pinch something because it would be exciting. You know that if you say no, your friend will look down on you and probably not speak to you. Do you do as they ask and take the item and keep your friendship?

HINT

A 'What if' scenario challenges the performers to consider an alternative ending to a piece of theatre. You will create two endings that show the consequences of making two different choices. Any varying choices in life will have a direct impact on the outcome of a situation.

a. Reconvene and discuss your responses to the dilemmas posed.
   Again in groups of four or five share your own personal dilemmas. These can be whatever each one of the group desires to share, big or small. Discuss any decisions that your fellow students have made and whether these are the decisions that other pupils in the group would have taken.

b. After you have shared your personal dilemmas, pick one that has sparked controversy within the groups. Using the chosen dilemmas, the group should then dramatise the story with a 'what if' scenario incorporated in the action.

c. Devise the actual ending of the piece, then also create an alternative ending which is the product of making a different choice in the scene. You must find a way to build the alternative choice and ending into the structure of the performance, acting one then returning to an appropriate place in the scene and acting the other.
   This illustrates how we often have multiple choices in the decisions we make, and how those choices influence how events unfold.

Exercise 2: The miners' strike

Police arresting a protestor at Orgreave, South Yorkshire at the 'Battle of Orgreave, 1984'

1. Place a chair in the middle of the room and the class should walk around the space. You should take turns in standing on the chair where you will proudly make a statement about something you do not agree with. This should encourage you as a group to bring up issues that are close to your hearts, and topics you feel passionately about.

   After each one of you has had a turn you should then state what you could do to resolve your issue. Find out in a class discussion if any of the class feel strongly against another pupil's issue. A conversation could follow if any of you disagree.

   This starter will now lead on to the introduction of the miners' strike of 1984, in which there was:

   ● Mass strike action up and down the country due to government plans to massively scale back the UK coal mining industry.

   ● Loss of jobs and the breaking-up of communities due to pit closures.

2. Discuss how you might react if you and your friends lived in a tight-knit community where you all worked together, but in which you all lost your jobs suddenly and out of the blue. Would you fight back, and if so, how?

3. Read through the extract below taken from *The Last Heroes* written by Nick Walker:

THE YEAR 1985 – MINERS' STRIKE

A POLICE LINE CHARGES ONTO THE FRONT OF THE STAGE FACING THE AUDIENCE AND MAKES A LINE. SMOKE IN THE AIR. CHANTS FROM OFF, BITS OF 'MAGGIE, MAGGIE, MAGGIE!'

POLICE 1:   Hold the line here, boys!

POLICE 2:   They're coming from the north side of town! Some flying pickets from Sheffield are coming in on the train.

POLICE 3:   If they're flying pickets, shouldn't they be able to hover in by themselves?

POLICE 1:   Keep concentrated!

SHOUTS FROM BEHIND THE AUDIENCE. POLICE BRACE THEMSELVES.

POLICE 1:   Batons ready!

POLICE 2:   Watch for missiles coming at us, some of the fencing has been torn up.

FROM THE BACK WE HEAR A VOICE SHOUT THROUGH. IT'S THE DAD AS A NINETEEN YEAR OLD, HE'S CALLED MACK.

MACK: Lovely day for a riot, isn't it?

POLICE 1:   Keep steady, it's just one man.

POLICE 2:   He could be the head of a pack.

MACK: We don't often get out in the sun, us miners. Wish I'd brought my Raybans.

POLICE 3:   What do we do with him?

POLICE 1:   Don't react, this is a bottleneck.

MACK COMES OUT AND STANDS SQUARE IN FRONT OF THE LINE OF POLICE.

MACK: Imagine breathing this fresh air every day of your working life. You lot ever thought what the air's like a hundred yards underground?

POLICE 1: Keep the line.

HE WALKS UP AND DOWN THE LINE.

MACK: Not very many of you are there? All full of oxygen and sunshine. Are you sure you'll be able to hold us back? There are thousands of us grubby bastards out today. Coal dust under our fingernails.

POLICE 2: Sarge.

POLICE 1: Stay calm.

MACK: I spit black, do you know that?

POLICE 1: Steady men.

MACK: You look like dominoes. One little push and you'll all be over.

POLICE 2: Is that a threat?

MACK: No, that's not a threat.

HE TURNS TO FACE THE AUDIENCE, HIS BACK TO THE POLICE.

MACK: This is a threat.

HE SHOUTS

MACK: Now lads!

THE LIGHTS GO OUT, SMOKE POURS IN AS IF THROWN BY SMOKE BOMBS AND A HAIL OF ROCKS IS HEARD BANGING OFF RIOT SHIELDS.

POLICE 1: Riot shields up high!

POLICE 2: Take the line back!

POLICE 3: Stay together!

POLICE 2: Pull back! All units pull back!

ONE POLICEMAN GETS STRANDED IN A SPOTLIGHT.

POLICE 4: Pull back to where? Pull back to where?

MACK APPEARS WITH AN IRON BAR. WE SEE HIM RAISE IT ABOVE HIS HEAD AND THE LIGHTS GO OUT. WE HEAR THE CRACKLE OF A POLICE RADIO.

RADIO: Are you there PC 347? PC 347, come in!

a. Discuss if you would attempt to solve a work or school dispute in the same way that Mack did. Would, or have, any of the pupils in your class resorted to violence in solving a problem?

b. Consider whether Mack felt that hitting the police officer was justified – bearing in mind that his job was being taken off him, the community that he lived in was being broken apart and the police were stood with riot shields and batons. Group all those who believe it was justified '1' and all those who disagree with Mack's actions '2'.

4. Those now numbered 1 are to write a monologue from the point of view of Mack. Consider the reasons behind Mack's decision to hit the police officer. They should write the monologue using these questions as a guide:

    - What were your reasons for resorting to violence?
    - Do you regret hitting the police officer?
    - Was the attack pre-meditated?
    - What were your feelings as you brought the iron bar down over the police officer's head?
    - Do you think that sacrificing a police officer's life is justified given the circumstances?
    - What was your immediate reaction to hitting the police officer?

    Those numbered '2' are to write a monologue from the perspective of a policeman involved in the scene above, but not the officer being hit by Mack. They should use these questions as a guide:

    - Do you agree with the miners' strike?
    - Were you scared as you faced the striking miners?
    - Do you want to cause the miners harm?
    - What do your family think of your job as a police officer stopping the miners?
    - What was your reaction to your colleague being hit by Mack?
    - Do you want revenge against Mack for the attack?

    As a class consider how you should structure a monologue. Consider how the scene is created and possibly use the structure and tension of the scene to influence your monologue.

The above exercise was adapted from The Belgrade Community & Education Company Education pack

5. Read the following first-hand account of a person who was against the miners' strike in 1984.

WHAT IS A SCAB?

When your father dies without talking to you for six years, it shows it wasn't just those bastards in the NUM affected by the strike.

He wouldn't speak to me because I was against Scargill; he would only speak to me through my brothers.

What is a scab? My interpretation of a scab is somebody crossing a picket line but there wasn't anything official about those picket lines set up in Nottinghamshire.

I have seen full grown men, hard men, crying their bloody eyes out because of the fear of going across them. People are never, ever going to forget that.

My daughter Colette was 10 at the time and I stopped her going out of the house. We didn't want to tell her somebody was threatening to kill her; threatening to burn our house down.

They threatened my wife, Sheila. One day 80 people gathered outside our house but I drove into the crowd and they dispersed.

We had a copper as a next door neighbour and he put a sign in his window saying 'Greatrex lives next door' because he was sick of bricks going through his window.

And they say let bygones be bygones. It is never going to happen, the bitterness is too ingrained.

At the time, I would think to myself: 'Am I doing right? Should I be doing this?'

a. In groups of four or five respond to the above account and use these questions as a guide to your discussion:
   - Do you agree with how this man behaved?
   - Was he right in what he did?
   - Do you agree with the action of the Policeman who was his next door neighbour?
   - What advice would you have given this man?
   - Where would you have been during the strike – with the picket lines or with the 'scabs'? Why?

b. Reconvene and share your thoughts. Do all the groups agree or disagree? In groups of four or five devise a scene between a group in a picket line and one or two miners who attempt to cross the picket line.

Exercise 3: Cyberbullying

Cyberbullying is when someone uses platforms on the Internet or mobile devices such as Twitter and Facebook to deliberately upset, insult or threaten someone else. This is a form of bullying and no one should put up with it.

By using technology like mobile phones, this type of bullying can affect someone not just at school, but at home as well. Because it takes place in the virtual world, it has a 24/7 nature and can make someone feel upset or threatened in their own home.

The nature of this type of bullying means it can have a large audience, many of whom may not realise they are being bullies.

1. Read the following news item:

ONE MESSAGE, LIVES FOREVER CHANGED

An alarming number of young people are being bullied today, and it's no longer limited to school.

The disturbing world of 'cyberbullying' is pushing kids over the edge.

Doctors diagnosed Megan Meier with depression and attention deficit disorder in the third grade.

Megan's mother, Tina Meier, said throughout school, bullies constantly targeted Megan because of her appearance.

'Megan, for so long, had such low self-esteem because of her weight', Meier told CBN News.

Eventually, Megan's parents decided to put her in private school. Tina said things got better.

'For eighth grade, though, she started blossoming, started smiling, and laughing', Meier recalled. 'She started working out and exercising and losing weight; feeling better about herself.'

However, three weeks before her fourteenth birthday party, a message on Megan's MySpace page gave her a jolt.

It came from a friend named Josh who Megan described as a boy who thought she was pretty.

'So Megan got on, and the message from Josh from the night before was, 'You heard me. No one likes you. No one wants to be friends with you', Meier explained.

The bullying then exploded with messages and bulletins going out to hundreds of kids.

'The messages were horrendous', Meier said. 'They were not just, "I don't like you anymore". They called Megan all kinds of horrible names, talking about her weight, the way that she looked, cursing. I mean using things that are unbelievable.'

It caused Megan to sob hysterically, and she ran to her room.

A short time later, the 13 year old committed suicide, hanging herself in her bedroom closet.

'Every single dream, every hope, everything she wanted to be was gone in two hours', her mother said. 'Two hours on a computer and that life that was so precious was gone.'

As a class discuss cyberbullying and give your responses to the above news story.

2. In groups of four or five devise a monologue for the mother in the above story using these questions as a guide:
    ● When did the mother first realise that Megan was depressed?
    ● How did she find out about the cyberbullying?
    ● Did she discuss this with Megan?
    ● Did the mother discuss Megan's problems with the school before moving her to a private school?
    ● How did she feel when she read the message from Josh?
    ● What are her feelings now following the death of Megan?

    After working on the monologue together, choose one of the group to present it to the other pupils.

3. In groups of four or five devise a scene where a group of friends discuss what is happening to a pupil in their class who is being cyberbullied? One of the group could be the bully, unknown to the others. Would he or she be found out? What would be the response of the others?

    After presenting your different scenes to the rest of the class, discuss the following questions:
    ● How are teenagers being cyberbullied?
    ● How do victims react?
    ● How can we prevent cyberbullying?
    ● What else can we do to stay cyber-safe?

Exercise 4: Jealousy

In groups of four or five discuss the following scenarios.

SCENARIO 1

Your best friend tells you that they've been given £300 for getting all Cs at GCSE, whereas you got all As and received nothing.

SCENARIO 2

You have secretly liked a particular individual for months, and you finally decide that you are going to tell them. Just as you are about to talk your best friend sweeps in and asks them out on a date.

SCENARIO 3

Your best friend does not do any work, but consistently gets higher grades than you. You have just received test results and they have again done better than you but on less work.

SCENARIO 4

Your friend's parents buy them a brand new car on their seventeenth birthday in preparation for them learning to drive. You have just found out.

SCENARIO 5

You're in a relationship with someone, and you notice them spending a lot of time with another individual who is known for breaking up relationships.

Each group should create a still image for each of these scenarios. After you have created your still images, discuss what feelings may be associated with these situations. Think of the idea of jealousy.

What is jealousy?

Jealousy is an emotion and typically refers to the negative thoughts and feelings of insecurity, fear, and anxiety over an anticipated loss of something that the person values, such as a relationship, friendship, or love. Jealousy often consists of a combination of emotions such as anger, sadness, and disgust.

1. As a class discuss if there has ever been a time when you have experienced jealousy. Every pupil should explain what it felt like.
2. In your groups, devise a scene around your chosen scenario.

The above exercise was adapted from The Belgrade Community & Education Company Education pack

Exercise 5: Friendship

1. As a class, think about your friendships and what makes those relationships work.
2. Next work in pairs and create two still images which represent a good friendship (i.e. a friendship that works and is long lasting). Think about how balanced the roles are in that relationship, how the power is distributed between the pairing, and whether there is equality in the relationship.
3. Next in pairs create two still images which represent a friendship that does not work. Think again how this affects equality, balance and power distribution in the relationship.
4. Consider in pairs how you treat your friends. Share your images and your thoughts with the rest of the class.
5. Read through these scenarios:

SCENARIO 1

Chris asks his friends to go to a dangerous place because he truly believes he has a mission to fulfil. He believes it is absolutely the right thing to do in order to fight evil. Is this a justifiable request to make of your friends?

SCENARIO 2

Chris joins in with karaoke and goes sky diving with his friends. He really gets involved in all the activities that his friends are involved in and is always the first to try something new. Is this a good trait of a friend?

SCENARIO 3

Chris' friend, Jay, comes to see him and tells him he has no money, Chris tells Jay not to worry as he can lend him money until he sorts himself out. Is this a good act by Chris? Is it right for Jay to ask?

SCENARIO 4

Whilst in a club, Chris starts an argument with the owner and refuses to stop arguing even when his friends ask him. He believes he is right. It starts a fight and all of Chris' friends are forced to join in. Was Chris right to do this?

SCENARIO 5

Chris knows that his friend Jay is going to betray him, but he allows him to do it anyway because he knows it will teach him and his friends around him a valuable lesson. Is this a good decision from a friend?

a. In groups of four or five choose one of the above scenarios. Then devise a scene around your chosen scenario.
    Perform your scenarios in front of the other members of your class.
b. When all the groups have performed discuss the following questions:
    *   Was Chris a good friend or not?
    *   Was he right to behave in the manner he did?
    *   How would you have behaved?
    *   Would you have given an alternative ending to one of the other scenes?

The above exercise was adapted from The Belgrade Community & Education Company Education pack

THEATRE IN EDUCATION

WHAT IS THEATRE IN EDUCATION? (OR TIE)

It starts with an educational topic or debate and develops a show around it

WHEN DID IT FIRST APPEAR AS AN ART FORM?

Back in 1965 in Coventry at the Belgrade Theatre

WHAT STEPS YOU SHOULD TAKE WHEN DEVISING YOUR OWN TIE PRODUCTION?

Decide on your target audience

Decide on a topic

Write your scene

Research your topic

Include audience participation

Evaluate your work

If I want to use the TIE genre in my devised piece I would:

Follow the steps shown above.

Pick 'n mix from the dramatic devices shown in Section 1, e.g. narrator, cross-cutting, multi-roling, thought tracking, direct address, flashbacks.

B. PHYSICAL THEATRE

What is Physical Theatre?

Physical Theatre is a form of acting that tells a story through the way bodies are positioned and the way they move forming different shapes. Physical Theatre uses our bodies for our effects rather than using props, scenery or even sound effects at times.

Physical Theatre can include a wide variety of styles and approaches – it can include dance-theatre, movement theatre, clown, puppetry, mime, mask, vaudeville and circus.

Physical Theatre-based companies

Today there are many companies in the UK who practise a physical or more movement-based style of theatre, for example:

DV8
a well-known group who have done many works classed as physical theatre.

TRESTLE
famous for their 'mask theatre'.

COMPLICITE
this company is based in London and uses extreme movement to represent their work.

FRANTIC ASSEMBLY
another well-known group who have done a lot of Physical Theatre and who have produced their own book on the genre.

EARTHFALL
one of Wales' leading Physical Theatre companies.

KNEEHIGH
they use a variety of theatrical elements including puppetry, live music and have an emphasis on visual imagery.

The following exercises will help you to understand how actors use movement, gesture and body language to show emotions or feelings, and how this allows them to convey different characters or to communicate their status to an audience.

Exercise 1

Walk around your rehearsal space, making sure that you walk in straight lines, turning every time you want to change direction. Your teacher will call out some commands and instructions and you are to respond quickly.

Commands could include:

- Pretend to hide in the room.
- Strike a model pose from a catalogue.
- Strut your stuff like you are on a catwalk.
- You are extremely afraid of something you have seen.
- You have just received some very bad news.
- Something has made you extremely happy.
- Show pride, shame, jealousy, vanity.

Exercise 2

a. Choose one of the occupations below and convey the character through movement, gesture and body language.
b. Repeat the exercise with another of the occupations.
    Each pupil should perform their actions in front of the others in the class.

FARMER   CLEANER   BUILDER

FLORIST   MECHANIC   HAIRDRESSER

BARMAID   PLUMBER   HOUSEWIFE

ELECTRICIAN

FIREMAN   WAITRESS   NURSE

SECRETARY

SOLDIER   PLUMBER

DECORATOR

SHOPKEEPER   TEACHER

Exercise 3

a. As an individual think of a machine or mechanical object and think how it would move. You'd expect most movements would be mechanical and machine-like.

   Get into groups of four or five with your individual machine-like movements and put these together in a sequence to make a sort of machine or production line. Try to alter the rhythms and speeds of the movements so that you are not all moving in the same way.

b. You could add sound to the movements. Each one of you should make a sound that he or she feels represents some part of the machine. Again remember to make contrasts in rhythms, tones, loud, soft, high and low, fast, slow, short and long to make the sound of the machine more interesting.

c. Show the machine you have created through movement and sound to the rest of the class.

Exercise 4

a. Individually choose one of the animals shown (or you can choose your own) and then move around the room as that animal.

   Exaggerate the movement features of the animal as much as you can.

b. When everyone has had a chance to work on their own try to pair up with a partner – either another pupil playing the same animal or a pupil playing a different animal.

   Take it in turns to tell each other what has happened to you. When communicating with each other the movements and sound could be exaggerated again.

   It should be gibberish rather than language.

   The more ridiculous you look and sound the better.

67

Exercise 5

The Waiter

You will need a table and a chair and a tea-towel. Two volunteers play this game, one is the waiter, who carries the tea-towel over their arm, and the other is the customer who comes to eat at the restaurant. Actors do not speak. Everything apart from the table, chair and tea-towel, is mimed. It is a posh, upmarket restaurant.

Do not decide anything else. Just play the game.

How the waiter carries/uses the tea-towel, how a particular actor enters spark ideas. Try not to impose anything. The humour emerges from the fact that both actors try very hard to get things right (including the mime). They fail of course!

Exercise 6

The letter

A blank sheet of paper folded into an envelope is the only prop you need. Place the letter onstage. A volunteer enters. He or she sees the letter and reacts and plays an imaginary situation physically and verbally. The letter isn't necessarily addressed to the recipient. It is entirely up to the actor who it is for and what is in it. The 'world' you create does not have to realistic.

Try to avoid telling us what is in the letter. 'Oh wow! I've won the lottery – great!' or 'She's leaving me. Oh, God. I can't live without her.' The less you let us know, the more you will arouse and create suspense, as in the following examples:

'I don't believe it. No. Yes. It says.... It's true.'

Or

'No. Please. Don't. Don't leave.'

This leaves the meaning open to possibilities.

Jacques Lecoq

In the genre of Physical Theatre one of the most famous characters is Jacques Lecoq (1921–1999). He was born in Paris in 1921 and was a famous French actor, mime and acting instructor. He is most famous for his methods on Physical Theatre, movement and mime. Jacques Lecoq is regarded as one of the twentieth century's most influential teachers of the physical art of acting.

Here are a few examples of the type of Physical Theatre exercises used by Lecoq.

Exercise 7

Melodrama – physicalising emotional states
As a group and in complete silence, improvise the moment of departure of one member of a family. The person enters the room and it is the last time you will see them, and they you. You decide on the circumstances of their departure. Why is this member of the family leaving? Focus on the silent dramatic tension between characters.

Exercise 8

Restaurant
One person is the waiter, and another is a customer. The goal is for the two individuals to try as hard as possible to act 'correctly' – that is to say to not attempt to mess things up. The audience, watching closely, focuses on the minor mishaps which actually combine to create the real comedy. After enough time, the client can be told to be 'burlesque' by performing minor, obvious mistakes – for example he could drop the menu on the floor, or try to shake the waiter's hand with his left hand. It is the waiter's job to try to normalise the situation. Eventually, the two roles switch.

Exercise 9

Limited spaces

Think of situations that involve being in very small spaces – for example being stuck in a lift or as a prisoner in a tiny cell.

In groups of four or five create some very short scenes which explore the idea of people being in close proximity to each other, and how people respond to being in limited spaces.

Exercise 10

For this exercise you will have to do some preparation as homework.

a. Think of the name, age and occupation of a character. A character who could exist in the present day and in this country. Also, think of three adjectives that describe your character, e.g. scary, practical, insecure.

    Try to find a suitable costume for your character.

b. If possible try to arrive at your lesson in costume and in character. Stand in a circle with the other pupils and introduce your characters to each other. Then begin work on your physicality. Start by walking as neutrally as possible in the space you have. Then start exploring in detail how your character moves.

    Some things to consider would be: the distance between your feet; the length of your stride; whether your feet are parallel or turned in or out; which part of your body do you lead with head, stomach or chest.

    Explore and then decide on the particular way your character moves. Be bold and definite with your physicalisations.

c. The next step would be to use these characters in simple improvisations – in groups of four or five. For example – **Waiting at the doctor's surgery** OR **arriving at the cinema and finding a seat**. These are good situations because they are often silent and involve interactions with the other characters. They provide a way of looking at the creation of a physical text.

    After completing the improvisation discuss this with the students who were watching the performances. Discuss the different characters they have seen and discuss how the physicality of a character informs an audience about their emotional state, occupation or status.

'Masks'

Masked work had a powerful influence on Lecoq's approach to performing. He was intrigued with the simple and direct way masks could amplify the physical aspects of a performer, and be used to communicate with all kinds of audiences.

There are two kinds of masks you can choose from: a neutral mask without expression or a mask that conveys a feeling or emotion (for example happy, sad, evil).

What can you learn by using a mask?

You know that you rely heavily on your face for expression. When this means of expression is removed – by wearing a mask – communication is at first very difficult. However, you will gradually begin to use your whole body for expression. What tends to be most fascinating for the audience is the way the performers' movements and body language seem to change the masks.

Exercise 11

In groups of four or five and all wearing masks, perform the following scenarios. Do so in silence.

a.   Several people pass an accident on the street, with various reactions. (Or pass by a beautiful garden, or an unusual statue, or anything out of the ordinary.)

b.   Two, three, or more people arrive one at a time in a crowded movie theatre, in which there are only two (or three or whatever) seats empty. (We should see each one look for a seat, locate one, and go to it. We should be able to tell how each feels about taking a seat next to a stranger, and how each feels about the next person sitting by them. We should also be able to tell what kind of movie it is.)

c.   Several strangers (or, alternatively, not strangers) watch a sporting event, not all rooting for the same team. (We should be able to tell who the 'opposing' fans are, and which team is winning.)

These actors in rehearsal are performing Commedia dell'Arte, an Italian form of theatre that is characterised by using masks.

The Frantic Assembly

One of the Physical Theatre-based companies referred to earlier was The Frantic Assembly. Although now based in London, it was first established in Swansea when the co-founders Scott Graham and Steven Hoggett were students at the university there in the early 1990s.

They even have their own book of ideas and approaches on the subject of Physical Theatre – 'book of devising theatre.'

It's a classic work in this area, and is full of ideas and practical exercises that could help improve your understanding of this genre. Here are some extracts from their book:

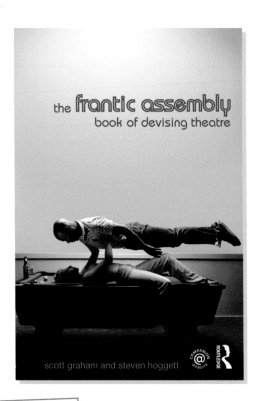

the **frantic assembly**
book of devising theatre

scott graham and steven hoggett

TIME PASSING

Think of a simple setting for two characters: on a sofa in front of a TV; in a cafe; a date in a restaurant. Ask your performers (or characters who inhabit the setting) to picture their moves over an extended period of time - all the changes of position and the different poses that one might get into quite naturalistically over the space of a couple of hours. If it helps to visualise it, think of a CCTV camera spying on the event and capturing the moves.

Get the two performers to set their individual moves, taking care to include moments of stillness and rest. If you then run the two individuals in the space, a physical story emerges. There may be moments that you want to hold on to, to set. Others you might want to change.

EYE CONTACT

Eye contact is such an important part of performance and theatre. When it happens you know you are being spoken to directly. There is no confusion and that recognition is instant. Yet it can be one of the more terrifying tasks for young practitioners and students to master.

SOME DOS AND DON'TS

DON'T make somebody become a table or chair that then gets sat on – this is not physical theatre, it is demeaning.

DON'T hold your breath when attempting particularly difficult physical movement – you need it. Breathe out during exertion.

DON'T STAND stock still facing the audience unless that really is what you mean to do.

DON'T stand back to back, link arms and lift one another by tilting forward – it doesn't mean anything. Honest.

**Reproduced with permission from 'The Frantic Assembly Book of Devising Theatre' by Scott Graham and Steven Hoggett . Routledge 2009

Activity

Using what you have learnt in this section and working in groups of four or five, devise your own scene that illustrates Physical Theatre.

You can use some sound, e.g. words or short sentences.

You can use masks.

The emphasis should be on movement, gestures and body language.

Use the following as a stimulus to your devised scene.

a) 'Skyfall' (Adele)
b) Sacrifice or Utopia

PHYSICAL THEATRE

WHAT IS PHYSICAL THEATRE?

A form of acting that tells a story through the use of movement, gesture and body language

PHYSICAL THEATRE-BASED COMPANIES

There are many companies practising a physical or more movement-based style of theatre

Through movement, gesture and body language you can convey different characters or communicate your status to an audience

Through movement, gesture and body language you can show different emotions and feelings

THE USE OF MASKS

The use of masks can amplify the physical aspects of a performer. Here we learnt of the work of Jacques Lecoq

If I want to use the Physical Theatre genre in my devised piece I would:

Include examples of showing emotions or feelings using movement, gesture and body language, in other words physicalising emotional states.

Experiment with the use of masks.

MUSICAL THEATRE

What is Musical Theatre?

Musical Theatre is a genre in which the story is told through the performance of singing, spoken dialogue and often dance. You need to understand, however, that it does NOT include all theatre that uses music. Musical Theatre excludes, for example, opera, ballet, dance shows and plays with music.

Although Musical Theatre is closely related to the theatrical form of opera, one important factor that distinguishes both is that Musical Theatre has a greater focus on spoken dialogue.

Famous examples of Musical Theatre

THE SOUND OF MUSIC

The Sound of Music is a musical with music by Richard Rodgers and lyrics by Oscar Hammerstein, and a book by Howard Lindsay and Russel Crouse. It is based on the memoir of Maria von Trapp, 'The Story of the Trapp Family Singers'.

The original Broadway production opened in November 1959. It was later adapted as a film in 1965 starring Julie Andrews and Christopher Plummer.

FIDDLER ON THE ROOF

The original Broadway production of the show, which opened in 1964, had the first Musical Theatre run in history to surpass 3000 performances. There was a successful film adaptation in 1971.

The story centres on Tevye, the father of five daughters, and his attempts to maintain his family and Jewish religious traditions while outside influences encroach upon their lives. He must cope both with the strong-willed actions of his three older daughters – each one's choice of husband moves further away from the customs of his faith – and with the edict of the Tsar that evicts the Jews from their village.

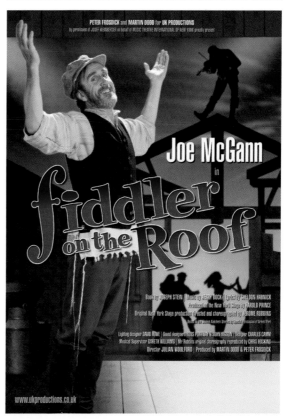

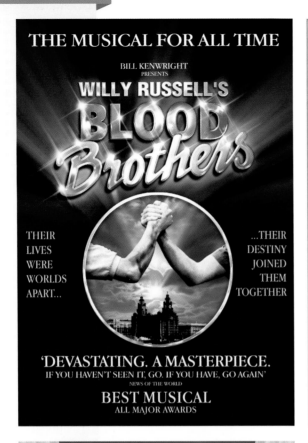

BLOOD BROTHERS

Blood Brothers is a musical with music, lyrics and a book by Willy Russell, based loosely on the 1844 novella *The Corsican Brothers* by Alexandre Dumas. The story is a contemporary nature versus nurture plot, revolving around fraternal twins who were separated at birth.

Originally developed as a school play, Blood Brothers opened in Liverpool before Russell transferred it to the West End for a short run in 1983. It went on a year-long tour before later returning to the West End in 1988. After transferring to the Phoenix Theatre in 1991, Blood Brothers spent more than 24 years in the West End, and played more than 10,000 performances, becoming the third longest-running musical production in West End history.

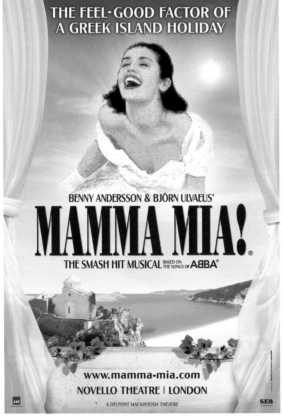

MAMA MIA

Mama Mia is based on the songs of Abba, the popular pop and dance group from Sweden, who were together and recording in the period from 1972 to 1982.

In 1997 the producer Judy Craymer commissioned Catherine Johnson to write the book for the musical. In 1998 Phyllida Lloyd became the director for the show and it opened in the West End at the Prince Edward Theatre in 1999 and transferred to the Prince of Wales Theatre in 2004, where it played until September 2012, when it moved to the Novello Theatre.

What are lyrics? **TIP**
Poetry that expresses subjective thoughts and feelings, often in a song-like style or form.

What are the main characteristics of Musical Theatre?

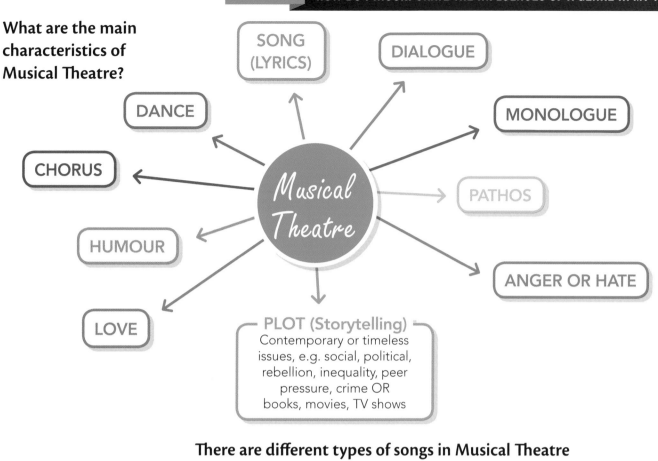

SONG (LYRICS)

DIALOGUE

DANCE

MONOLOGUE

CHORUS

PATHOS

Musical Theatre

HUMOUR

ANGER OR HATE

LOVE

PLOT (Storytelling)
Contemporary or timeless issues, e.g. social, political, rebellion, inequality, peer pressure, crime OR books, movies, TV shows

There are different types of songs in Musical Theatre which are integral to the structure of the plot:

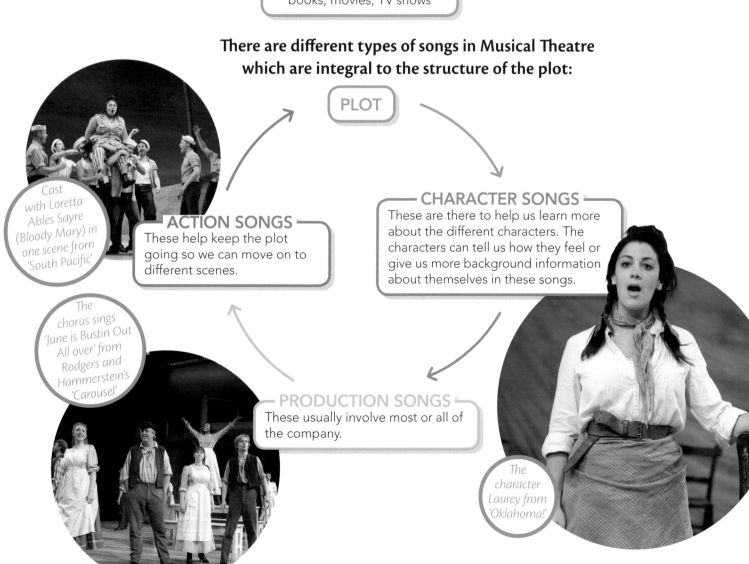

PLOT

Cast with Loretta Ables Sayre (Bloody Mary) in one scene from 'South Pacific'

ACTION SONGS
These help keep the plot going so we can move on to different scenes.

CHARACTER SONGS
These are there to help us learn more about the different characters. The characters can tell us how they feel or give us more background information about themselves in these songs.

The chorus sings 'June is Bustin Out All over' from Rodgers and Hammerstein's 'Carousel'

PRODUCTION SONGS
These usually involve most or all of the company.

The character Laurey from 'Oklahoma!'

Exercise 1

It's not easy to write an original song. Therefore for this first exercise let's imitate existing songs.

a. In groups of four or five, select a song you are familiar with. It could be a song from the present charts, or a classic you all know.

b. As a group, choose a topic which will be the basis for your song lyrics. Because storytelling is a characteristic of Musical Theatre, the more conflict, the better. Here are a few suggestions:

- Your boyfriend/girlfriend has left you for someone new.
- Your parents refuse to let you go to a disco with your friends.
- You find out that one of your friends is talking about you behind your back.
- You have been wrongly accused of shoplifting.

c. As a group, write as many of the lyrics as you can, and set them to the tune of your chosen song. Your lyrics should tell a story or convey a lyrical dialogue.

The song can be presented to the rest of the class either by simply reading the lyrics, or if someone of the group is brave enough, they can perform the newly created song.

Exercise 2

a. In groups of four or five, choose one of the group to play **impromptu** music, using a simple keyboard, while the other members of the group perform.

There is no need for the music to be anything special – just some basic music to convey different emotions.

Choose a location for your performance, e.g. library, youth club, leisure centre, surgery, office, etc.

The actors begin the scene with a normal, everyday dialogue.

- Hello Jared, did you enjoy the book?
- What's in store for us today, I wonder?
- I am getting tired of these fitness classes.

b. Once the conversation is underway, the member of the group playing the keyboard starts playing background music. This can alternate between dramatic, **whimsical**, romantic and so on.

The actors then must create action and dialogue that matches the mood of the music. Whenever the music changes, the behaviour of the characters changes.

Exercise 3

Find a soundtrack of 'Someone like You' by Adele. As a class, listen to the song. Adele wrote this song after she found out her ex-boyfriend was recently engaged to someone new.

In groups of four or five use this song as the basis for a devised scene.

a. Create a context for the song. Think of the situation suggested by the words. Write a dialogue and/or monologue leading up to the song. What would her feelings be now that she knows that her ex-boyfriend has 'settled down' and found someone new?

b. The words suggest that the girl in the song turned up 'uninvited' at the home of the ex-boyfriend. What would be the exchange between them? Would they remember the 'time of our lives'? How would the boyfriend feel when he hears from the girl that, for her, 'it isn't over'?

c. How would you create a scene with dialogue and song, using some of the words in Adele's song? Is there an outcome following the song? Does the situation change as a result of the song?

d. Write a dialogue and/or monologue to end the scene.

e. When performing the scene in front of the class, one of the group could attempt to sing the words or some of them. You could have more of the group join in singing some of the words. Alternatively, for this exercise, mime the words.

> **— REMEMBER —**
> When devising your own musical scene there is no need to be concerned that you are not a singer or that you are unable to compose your own music. You can always use existing songs and base your story around these.
>
> A good example of this is the musical referred to earlier, 'Mama Mia'. This musical was based on the songs of Abba. A story was created around the lyrics, and dialogue was used between the different songs.
>
> Remember too that songs in musicals play a crucial role in character and narrative development and arise naturally out of the story.

Exercise 4

In groups of four or five, look at this painting – Sir Patrick Spens by Elizabeth Eleanor Siddal. Devise a short musical scene based on that image.

a. Decide on the story that the picture conveys.

b. Think of 2–3 existing songs that would help to convey your story.

Choose appropriate music that could accompany your movements.

c. Decide on the dialogue and/or monologue that could be used.

d. Decide on dance movements that would enrich your performance.

The scene should last not more than 20–25 minutes.

e. Perform your devised scene in front of the other members of your class.

Almost anything can inspire a musical!

It was William Shakespeare who wrote the play '*Romeo and Juliet*'. But in 1957 this story inspired the creation of the famous musical '*West Side Story*.' And although it was Charles Dickens who created Oliver and Fagin, he didn't write the songs 'Food Glorious Food ' and 'Consider Yourself', which appeared in the hit musical '*Oliver*', inspired by Dickens' novel.

We mustn't forget either that Andrew Lloyd Webber based '*The Phantom of the Opera*' – one of the most successful stage musicals of all time – on a French novel which was originally published in 1909.

'*The Sound of Music*' is based on the real life memoir of Maria Von Trapp.

`79`

Exercise 5

In groups choose one of the following:

The Story of Gladys Aylward or *Out of the Ashes* (Michael Morpurgo)

1. Devise your own Musical Theatre based on your chosen text.
    a. You can concentrate on one section of the story. Create your own dialogue and/ or monologues.
    b. Decide on the songs you want to use – either existing songs that suit your story, or imitate existing songs, or write your own lyrics and music.
    c. Use music as background to your story. Search for suitable music. Also think about using dance/movement.
    d. The scene should last not more than 20–25 minutes.
    e. Perform your scene in front of other members of your class.

THE STORY OF GLADYS AYLWARD

The story begins with Gladys Aylward being rejected as a potential missionary to China because of her lack of education. Dr Robinson, the senior missionary, feels sorry for her and secures her a position in the home of a veteran explorer with contacts in China. Over the next few months, Aylward saves her money to purchase a ticket on the Trans-Siberian railway, choosing the more dangerous overland route to the East because it is less expensive.

Once in China, she settles in the town of Yang Cheng, where she secures a post as assistant to a veteran missionary, Jeannie Lawson, who has set up an inn for travelling merchants, where they can get a hot meal and hear stories from the Bible. Aylward takes over the inn when Lawson dies in an accident.

The local mandarin appoints Aylward, a stubborn but endearing woman, as his foot inspector to ensure that the ancient practice of foot binding is eradicated in the region he governs. She succeeds in this, and manages to put down a prison revolt as well, winning her the esteem of the local population as well as of the mandarin. Meanwhile, however, China is being invaded by Japan, and Aylward is encouraged by Lin to leave. She refuses, and as the town of Yang Cheng comes under attack, she finds that she has fifty orphans in her care.

As the population prepares to evacuate the town, the mandarin announces that he is converting to Christianity to honour Aylward and her work (she is rather taken aback by this, as she would have preferred him to convert through religious conviction). She is now left alone with the children, aided by Li, the former leader of the prison revolt that she helped to resolve. Li tells her that the only hope for safety is to take the children to the next province, where trucks will drive them to safety, but they must get there within three weeks, or else the trucks will leave without them.

Just as they are preparing to leave, another fifty orphans appear from a neighbouring town, so Aylward and Li have no choice but to lead one hundred children on a trek across the countryside. Although it should only have taken them a week, the roads are infested with Japanese patrols, and the group has no choice but to cut across the mountains. After a long, difficult journey, they all arrive safely (except for Li, who died to save them from a Japanese patrol) on the day the trucks are to leave. Aylward is greeted by Dr. Robinson, whom she reminds how he rejected her as a missionary years before.

News

OUT OF THE ASHES

This is not a story at all. It all happened. On New Year's Day Becky Morley begins to write her diary. By March, her world has changed for ever. Foot and mouth disease breaks out on a pig farm hundreds of miles from the Morely's Devon home, but soon the nightmare is a few fields away. Local sheep are infected and every animal is destroyed. Will the Morley's flock be next? Will their pedigree dairy herd, the sow with their piglets, and Little Josh, Becky's hand-reared lamb, survive? Or will they be slaughtered too? The waiting and hoping is the most agonising experience of Becky's life.

Michael Morpugo on stage in 2013 answering questions about his work.

Exercise 6

Extract from an existing musical: Disco Inferno, by Justin Sepple

---

Scene 4 INSIDE JANE'S HOUSE, LATER THAT EVENING

(Jane is sitting on the sofa still crying. Tom, Maggie and Terry are sitting with her.)

Maggie: You sit there and I'll make us all a cup of tea.

Tom: I'll give you a hand.

(Terry sits next to Jane)

Jane: What went wrong, Ter? We used to be so happy. (She cries) All I ever wanted was to settle and maybe have a family one day.

Terry: And you will...you're going to meet someone else, someone who cares a lot more about you than Jack. I know this is hard but you're not alone. We're all here for you. (He takes her hand)

(Knock at the door)

Jack: (O/S) Jane! Jane! We need to talk.

Jane: (To Terry) I don't want to see him.

Terry: Don't worry, I'll get rid of him.

Jack: (O/S) What are you doing here?

Terry: (O/S) What you should be doing...looking after Jane.

Jack: (O/S) Get out of my way. I want to talk to her.

(Jane is getting upset by the offstage argument. She covers her ears. Jack enters followed by Terry.)

Jack: Jane, we've got to talk. You don't look well. What's wrong?

Jane: Like you care.

(Tom and Maggie enter)

Jane: (Angry and upset) Please go, Jack.

Jack: At least give me a chance to explain.

Terry: Leave it, mate.

Jack: This has nothing to do with you...mate. I just want a moment alone with Jane.

Maggie: Jane?

Jane: Don't go anywhere.

Jack: (Calmly and meaningfully) Jane...I love you. I've always loved you. Just took my time saying it that's all.

Jane: (After deliberate hesitation) It's too late, Jack. It's too late. You have been so preoccupied with everything else...

Jack: You know just how hard I've been working - for our future - together.

Jane: Is that what you were doing with Kathy that night? Well that certainly clears that up.

Jack: It wasn't like that and you know it.

Jane: I know what I saw.

Jack: I'm always the one in the wrong, aren't I?

Jane: Oh, so it's my fault now is it? I can't believe I'm hearing this. I'm not the one who played around. It wouldn't be so bad if...just for once...you could admit that you made a mistake. But, O no, not you!

Jack: It's not my fault.

Jane: It never is. Just leave me alone.

Jack: We can't just throw away the past six years. You said we'd always be together.

Jane: That was before. Jack please go. You're only making things worse.

Jack: (shouting) Making things worse? How could they possibly get any worse?

Jane: (calmly) Just listen to me. It's over. Now please, just go away.

(Dejected, Jack steps forward into a spot)

SORRY SEEMS TO BE THE HARDEST WORD

Jack

What have I got to do to make you love me?

What have I got to do to make you care?

What do I do when lightnin' strikes me

An' I wake to find you're not there?

What have I gotta do to make you want me?

What have I gotta do to be heard?

What do I say now it's all over?

An' sorry seems to be the hardest word.

It's sad, so sad

> It's a sad situation
>
> And it's getting more and more absurd, oh my
>
> It's sad, so sad
>
> Why can't we talk it over?
>
> Always seems to me that sorry seems to be the hardest word.
>
> And sorry seems to be the hardest word.
>
> (c) 2004 Disco Inferno, Justin Sepple

1. In groups devise a scene to follow the one you have just read.
   Some ideas you could use:
   - What will Jack do now?
   - What will Jane do next?
   - Will Jack start a relationship with Kathy?
   - Will there be a confrontation between Jane and Kathy?
   - Will the conflict between Jack and Terry continue?
   - Has Jane another boyfriend that Jack doesn't know about?
   - Do Jack and Jane meet again and rekindle their relationship?

2. As an alternative you could use a different song from the 1970s
   as the stimulus for your devised scene.
   Here are some suggestions:
   - Somebody to Love (Queen)
   - Save Your Lovin For Me (Foghat)
   - You and I (Stevie Wonder)
   - Killing Me Softly With His Song (Roberta Flack)
   - You Really Got Me (Van Halen)
   - Don't Give Up On Us Baby (David Soul)

Roberta Flack (1937 –) achieved major commercial success in the 1970s with her version of the Fox/Gimbel hit Killing me Softly With His Song.

Exercise 7

This is a war poem by Studdert Kennedy:

> **Waste**
>
> Waste of Muscle, waste of Brain,
> Waste of Patience, waste of Pain,
> Waste of Manhood, waste of Health,
> Waste of Beauty, waste of Wealth,
> Waste of Blood, and waste of Tears,
> Waste of Youth's most precious Years,
> Waste of Ways the Saints have trod,
> Waste of Glory, waste of God,- War!

Devise a musical scene in response to the above poem: You could use the following ideas:

- The atrocities of war
- A conscientious objector
- For and against war
- Personal experiences of war (search the Internet for examples)
- You could include war songs (search the Internet for examples)
- Include dance/movement
- Remember your dramatic devices from Section 1, e.g. narrator, direct address, monologue, thought tracking, chorus, etc.

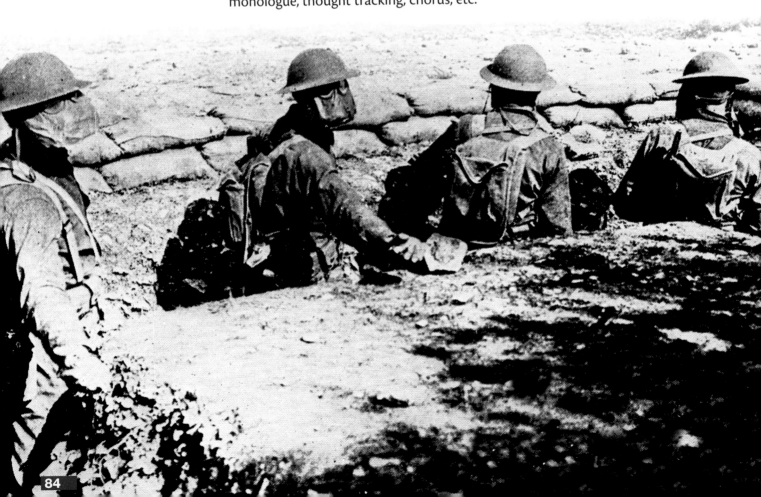

MUSICAL THEATRE

WHAT IS MUSICAL THEATRE?

A thatrical genre in which a story is told through singing, dialogue and dance

Musical Theatre does not include all theatre that uses music

THERE ARE DIFFERENT TYPES OF SONGS WHICH ARE INTEGRAL TO THE STRUCTURE OF THE PLOT

Action songs
Character songs
Production songs

MAIN CHARACTERISTICS OF MUSICAL THEATRE

Dialogue
Song
Dance
Humour
Monologue
Pathos
Anger or hate
Love
Chorus
Plot

If I want to use the Musical Theatre genre in my devised piece I would:

Include examples of dialogue, song and dance.

Include examples of different types of songs.

HOW DO I PERFORM MY DEVISED SCENE?

WHAT WILL I LEARN?

- In this section you will learn certain techniques to help you to give a better performance in your devised scene, which will be the sort of things your examiner is looking for.

1. Get to know your character

If you have a character to portray in your devised scene you should get to know the character thoroughly. There are certain questions you should ask yourself about the character:

1. Who am I?
Name, age, occupation, physical health, place of origin, status, characteristics, etc.

2. Where am I?
Outside/inside, room, building, city, country, etc.

3. When is it?
Hour, month, season, year.

4. What are my relationships?
To the place, to the other characters, etc.

5. What has happened before?
Events that took place in the character's life before the devised scene began, etc.

Exercise 1

- Choose one of these characters in the pictures below.
- Write a short biography for your chosen character, using the questions above to guide you.
- After writing your biography and learning it, tell your character's life story to the rest of the class.
- Using the technique of hot seating (see Section 1) allow yourself to be interrogated by the rest of the class. You should answer their questions in character.

2. Motivation

As well as the more obvious features of your character listed in 1 above, another less obvious but equally important aspect in getting to know your character is 'motivation'. But what is motivation? Well it can mean WHY someone is behaving in the way they do. If you apply it to your character, thinking about their motivation would mean:

- Why is your character there?
- Why is your character speaking?
- Why do they say what they do?
- What their intentions are at a particular moment in the scene.

Your character's motivation can change during the scene, and the same principle applies to our daily lives. For example, a person's original motivation is to go into town to do some shopping, but on the way they get a puncture. Now their motivation has switched to getting the tyre fixed.

Exercise 2

This simple exercise will help you understand motivation.

- As a class, take your turn to imagine that you are entering a room. Give three reasons why you are entering that room.
- In the same way – imagine that you are leaving the room. Give three reasons for your exit.
- All the time you're performing the exercise it's a good idea to have the word WHY in your head.

3. Learn your lines

The chances are that in your devised scene you will have lines to learn. For some students memorising will be a simple task. For others it can be a very difficult process indeed. This section will give you some handy hints if you find it difficult to read and remember your lines.

- Sir Anthony Hopkins, the famous Welsh film actor, writes his lines down. He writes each line three times. By the third time, he feels he's committed the line to memory.
- Repeat your lines over and over again. Try standing in front of a mirror and saying the lines. This way you can see what your face and body are doing as you say the lines.
- Stand up with your script and just start acting as you would do in your devised scene. This allows you to get the feel of the character. Associating words with actions can be a big help.
- Record yourself reading out your lines but make sure the recording is clear. You don't even have to be in character, read in monotone if you wish. Then listen to yourself on tape.
- Run through your lines with a friend or a member of the family. It doesn't matter if they're an actor or not. What's important is that they can tell you if you've missed out a few words and so on.

There are 10 things to remember in this section: **TIP**

Make sure you can recite all 10 of them, and why each is important.

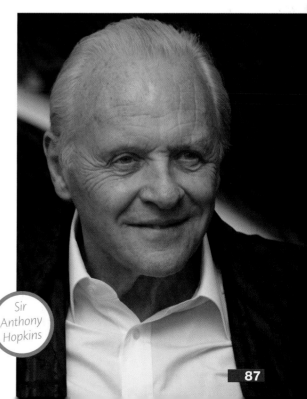

Sir Anthony Hopkins

And if you do forget your lines during a performance don't freeze. Instead try and remember the five DON'Ts:

DON'T	**DON'T**	**DON'T**	**DON'T**	**DON'T**
get flustered!	look out to the audience!	look towards your teacher!	look towards the prompt corner!	call out, 'Prompt!'

Stay in character. Keep the scene going to the best of your ability, and with the help of your fellow cast members hopefully you will get back on track.

In an exam you have only one chance to impress the examiner!

Exercise 3

In order to train your memory and give yourself the best chance in your devised performance, choose one of the following monologues and as homework learn the lines. Try learning it within a week. Then present the monologue to the rest of the class, and do your best to present the lines without having any prompts.

MAN: All right, look ... I didn't want to tell you, but I've fallen behind. At work. I can't keep up. Recently, they've ... ahh ... they've let a few people go. Every day there are fewer and fewer people doing the same amount of work. They have me running the accounting department entirely by myself! Not management, no, I haven't been promoted. It's just me – there's no one to manage! I do everything! The whole department! And that's not all! I'm also expected to take incoming calls because there's no receptionist, fix the computers because there's no tech department, field customer complaints because there's no customer service! I'm in charge of the mail room, the cafeteria, janitorial services, research and development! Last week, human resources was let go, the whole department, and I received a memo – which I'd actually typed myself because there's no secretary – instructing me to familiarise myself with all applicable state and federal guidelines! Tomorrow, I'm supposed to start mediating all employee disputes! I have no idea what I'm doing! I'd ask the legal department for advice, but I've never studied law so I wouldn't know what to tell myself! And to top it all off, I have to take the CEO's dog out to poop four times a day! At regular intervals! He has stomach problems and he's on a very strict schedule!

'The Worker' by Walter Wykes (left).

LADY BRACKNELL: Well, I must say, Algernon, that I think it is high time that Mr Bunbury made up his mind whether he was going to live or die. This shilly-shallying with the question is absurd. Nor do I in any way approve of the modern sympathy with invalids. I consider it morbid. Illness of any kind is hardly a thing to be encouraged in others. Health is the primary duty of life. I am always telling that to your poor uncle, but he never seems to take much notice ... as far as any improvement in his ailment goes. Well, Algernon, of course if you are obliged to be beside the bedside of Mr Bunbury, I have nothing more to say. But I would be much obliged if you would ask Mr Bunbury, from me, to be kind enough not to have a relapse on Saturday, for I rely on you to arrange my music for me. It is my last reception, and one wants something that will encourage conversation, particularly at the end of the season when everyone has practically said whatever they had to say, which, in most cases, was probably not much.

'*The Importance of Being Earnest*' by Oscar Wilde

Rupert Everett, Dame Judi Dench and Reese Witherspoon in the film version of 'The Importance of Being Earnest' (2002)

4. Don't fidget

It's more than possible that you will be nervous when performing your devised scene – especially in front of an examiner. Be aware of what you do when you are nervous, and try to avoid the following:

- Flick or play with your hair
- Scratch
- Rock on your feet
- Shuffling your feet
- Hiding your hands in your sleeves.

The only reason you'd do any of those things is if it were being used to indicate your character.

5. Concentration and involvement

If you lose concentration during your performance and break out in a giggle or a laugh (which is not part of your character) then you will lose marks!

During your performance never look directly at any member of the audience and there should be no eye contact with the examiner. Doing so will suggest a lack of **involvement** and you will lose marks. Of course an exception to this would be if you have chosen the dramatic device of addressing the audience directly, or you have chosen to use some of the techniques of Brecht. For a recap on this, see Sections 1 and 2.

6. Use of voice

The examiner will give you marks for your use of pace, pause, pitch and accent. All of these show your understanding of the role you play in your devised scene. Above all, clarity of speech is absolutely vital. So it is important that you do not rush your lines, that you do not mumble, or rush because you are nervous and so try to get it over with as quickly as possible.

It's just as important not to slow down too much, because in the end you could sound robotic and will bore the examiner and audience! Just think how your character would actually deliver the words you and the group have written.

Exercise 4

Try these tongue twisters to help you reach clarity of speech:

- Round the rugged rocks the ragged rascal ran
- Peter Piper picked a peck of pickled peppers
- Frenzied fleas fly frantically forward.
- Quick quotes quell querulous questions.

Start off slowly, and gradually build up until you say them at normal conversation speed. When speaking them, exaggerate the words, making your tongue, jaw and lips work hard. As you become surer of them, begin to **project** your **voice** and exaggerate the words more.

HINT

When you actually act in your devised performance, you can't emphasise each consonant to the same degree that you did with the tongue twisters. Using these is simply an exercise for practising purposes.

Pace is important!

You can vary the pace of your delivery. Some lines will be delivered quite slowly, others quicker. Again it depends on your character – and his or her motivation.

In the same way, it is important for you to vary tone and volume of speech. The examiner will mark you down if you speak in the same way for the whole scene, i.e. boring and monotonous.

Projection

You should speak loudly enough to be heard, without having to strain. Remember to use a range of volume in relation to the script.

Without yelling, you should make sure that your voice is loud enough to be heard in the back of the theatre. This is what is known as projection. When you are not projecting your voice, it's because you are speaking to a space right in front of your face. Projection means that you focus on a point farther away.

When you practise your devised scene, practise speaking to various objects in the room. Start with something close, like a chair. Then when you think that the chair is hearing you, focus on something a little farther away, until in the end you focus on something that is across the room from you, on the farthest wall.

BUT if you feel your voice straining, stop, don't force it. Even if your character is speaking quietly, or using a 'stage whisper', this again should be loud enough for everyone to hear clearly what you are saying.

7. Emphasis

What is emphasis? Emphasis is the stress laid on a word or words to indicate special meaning or particular importance. Think very carefully about the subtext of each line you deliver, and emphasise accordingly.

What is subtext? Subtext is thoughts not expressed directly in the text such as emotions and tension. It is the unspoken content that sits under the spoken dialogue.

Emphasis can play an important role in anything you say. Emphasis can change the meaning of any words you deliver. Take this simple sentence, for example:

'I didn't think it was you.'

If we emphasise different words in that sentence, it can change its meaning every time:

I didn't think it was you

I *didn't* think it was you

I didn't *think* it was you

I didn't think it *was* you

I didn't think it was *you*!

Exercise 5

In the same way, experiment with the following sentences:

- Could it be any different?
- It couldn't happen to anybody else.
- How can I hope to make you understand?

The actor Brian Blessed (1936–) is one of the most well-known contemporary actors who demonstrate incredible projection.

8. Variety

It was emphasised earlier that during your devised performance it is very important to vary tone, pace, pitch and volume. This variety helps your performance to be more interesting and more engaging. Here are a few exercises to help you gain such variety.

Exercise 6

This exercise will help you to see that there are an infinite number of ways of saying the same thing, and that it is the way that we say them that alters the meaning.

As a class, sit in a circle (with your teacher). The teacher will give an instruction such as **LOUDLY** and everyone must say their name as loudly as possible. The teacher will then change the instruction a number of times to explore different vocal skills, such as **WHISPERING**, where you and the other pupils must whisper but still be heard, then **QUICKLY** and **SLOWLY** to explore pace.

The exercise can be developed further so that instead of just saying your name you and the other pupils will say a phrase such as 'I can't wait' with different emotions to explore how vocal tone changes meaning. The teacher will use instructions such as **ANGRILY, BORED, SURPRISED, SAD, EXCITED, SARCASTIC**, etc. See how the volume and pace change with the different emotions as well as the tone.

Other phrases you could experiment with are:

- **'I'd love to'**

- **'Let's meet up soon'**

- **'I'm happy to help'**

- **'Thank you so much'**

Exercise 7

Work in pairs and sit/stand opposite each other. The teacher will give the class a theme for a conversation such as having an argument, winning the lottery, the death of a pet hamster, etc. In pairs begin to converse on this theme. The rule, however, is that you must talk gibberish for the whole time whilst trying to convey what you mean. Good examples will show how pupils are using their voices, making it clear what the conversation is about, without the use of words.

Exercise 8

Stay in pairs. You are going to take it in turns to deliver a one-minute monologue to your partner, on a theme given by the teacher. You should try to vary the way you speak through the monologue using different volume, pace and tone. You could base the stories on reality, but also add in extra moments or exaggerate for effect.

Themes could be:

- What I did at the weekend
- My last birthday party
- The best holiday I ever had

[The three exercises above were adapted from the active 8 theatre website: active8theatre@googlemail.com]

9. Movement and space

The examiner will look carefully at your use of movement and space. If used sensitively and in a very disciplined manner, you will gain more marks.

Movement

Getting to know your character thoroughly means you will know exactly how they move. Your body language, gestures and moves should indicate both your mood and character.

- How do you walk?
- How do you sit down?
- What mannerisms do you have?

Your movement within the acting area is very important. Some of you move about a lot, others not so much, but even if you are sitting in a chair you can still show reactions and responses by how you use the chair. Use your body even more here – be aware of your restricted movement and pay more attention to your face and hands.

All movements should appear natural and spontaneous – NOT pre-planned and rigidly worked out. Such movements will be deemed mechanical!

> **HINT**
>
> Variety in tone, pitch, and pace is very important if you choose Brecht as your practitioner. Your use of voice will change depending on whether you are in character or addressing the audience.
>
> The same applies if you choose Theatre in Education as your genre. There will be occasions during the scene where you will come out of character and again directly address the audience. In doing so your use of voice will vary.

> —— **REMEMBER** ——
>
> Keep in character ALL the time, even when you are not speaking or moving.

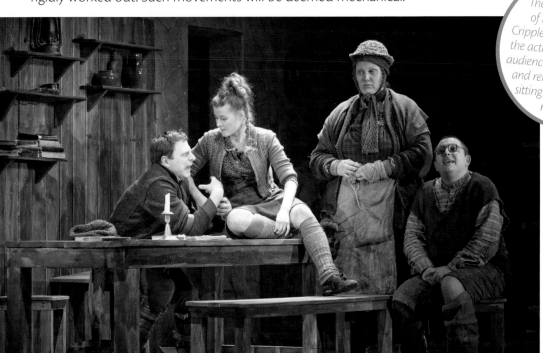

A Taganka Theatre performance of McDonagh's 'The Cripple from Inishmaan'. All the actors are in view of the audience, all are in character and remain so even if just sitting at the edge of the main action.

Exercise 9

In pairs look at the following **scenario** and discuss how you would perform this situation using movement without words.

A man or woman is at home.

They are due to leave for a very important meeting.

They want to look their best – and make sure of that before leaving the house.

The phone rings. They are unsure whether to answer it or not. After some deliberation they pick up the receiver.

It's obvious that they have had some bad news. They look at their watch. They are due to leave shortly. They decide to replace the receiver – unsure what to do next.

Eventually they decide to leave and look for their car keys. They can't find them. They panic. They frantically search everywhere for them. Unable to find them they sit down on the sofa.

They try to decide what to do next. Suddenly they spot the keys – they were not in their usual place.

They quickly collect their things ready to leave but they still think of that disturbing phone call. They go back to the phone and consider phoning but at the last moment they decide against it.

They rush for the door but as they are about to leave the phone rings. They turn – and then what do they do?

One of you should perform the situation and the other can stop the performance at any moment and suggest a change in gesture or movement.

Exercise 10

In pairs look at the following situation and perform it using body language, gestures and moves – do the whole performance without using words.

> They are sitting patiently in a coffee shop. It is obvious that they are waiting for somebody. Look at their watch. Start to get impatient.
>
> At last the friend arrives. They haven't seen each other for some time.
>
> They start a conversation – and everything seems fine.
>
> Suddenly one of them says something that obviously upsets the other.
>
> They start an argument and as time goes on the argument gets very heated.
>
> How does the scene end?

Space

When considering space you must decide on the type of stage you will use for your devised scene – and the position of the audience.

You could choose from the following:

Four types of stage

Proscenium arch

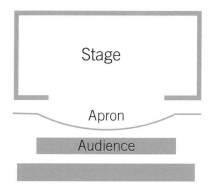

Thrust

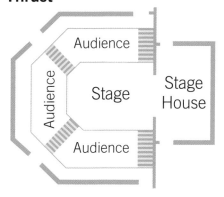

Traverse

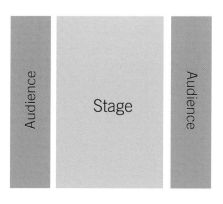

In the round

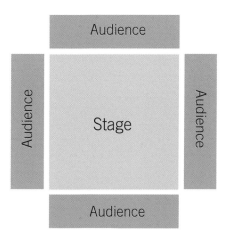

HINT

If you choose the genre Physical Theatre for your devised scene, remember that it is a form of acting that tells a story through the way bodies are positioned, and the way they move forming different shapes.

Physical Theatre uses the body for effects rather than using props, scenery or even sound effects at times.

10. Interaction

The examiner will award marks for excellent interaction with other characters. This means listening and responding to what they are saying and doing in their characters on stage:

- Always listen to what others say in the scene. Show that your response is a result of a thought, not just a line of dialogue.
- Always work as a team with others, pulling together to perform your scene.
- Remember to respond physically and facially as well as verbally – even though you may not have any lines to say at any one time, you should still be reacting, and very likely the examiner will be watching you during this time.

Understanding the practitioner and genre

Finally when devising your scene and choosing your practitioner and genre make sure that you have a full understanding of both.

This brings us back to the first sections of this book. Remind yourself about the techniques of Brecht, Stanislavski and Boal. Why are they so different?

When you choose your genre, remind yourself of the differences between Physical Theatre, Theatre in Education and Musical Theatre. What makes them different?

The examiner will award marks for an excellent understanding of your chosen practitioner or genre and will look for a very sophisticated final performance.

PHYSICAL THEATRE

MUSICAL THEATRE

THEATRE IN EDUCATION

HOW TO PERFORM

TECHNIQUES TO HELP YOU GIVE A BETTER PERFORMANCE IN **YOUR DEVISED SCENE**

Don't fidget

Know your character

Movement and Space

Motivation

Variety

Learn your lines

Concentration and Involvement

Interaction

Use of voice

Emphasis

HOW DO I WRITE AN EVALUATION OF MY DEVISED SCENE?

WHAT WILL I LEARN?

O **How to write an effective evaluation of your devised scene for exam purposes.**

After you have performed your devised scene you will be expected to write a 1500-word written report of the whole process, from beginning to end. This is an important part of your Unit 1 exam and the examiner will look out for a detailed explanation of the whole process.

The written report is divided into three parts:

1. Rationale
2. Development
3. Performance.

WHAT DO I INCLUDE IN EACH PART?

Rationale

1. Your choice of stimulus and the reasons for it. Refer to the different stimuli presented to you by the teacher. These can be either an image, a poem, a song, a news item, an extract from a play or just an idea, e.g. nightmare. Make sure that you refer to the discussions within your group regarding each stimulus and your reasons for choosing one of them for your devised piece. The image or picture, for example, captured your imagination and it conveyed a special atmosphere that you could develop into an effective piece of theatre.

This is an example of a possible opening paragraph:

COMMENT ①
Give examples of the stimuli you were given.

COMMENT ②
Show the examiner that you discussed the different stimuli as a group.

COMMENT ④
Identify your choice of stimulus.

> When we started our devised practical work our teacher gave us a selection of stimuli to choose from which would be the basis of our devised scene.
> We were shown a picture entitled Parsifal by the artist Anselm Kiefer, a news headline 'Teens arrested over Facebook Prank', the word Nightmare and a poem by Wilfred Owen, the war poet. We discussed each one in turn and could see possibilities in more than one of them but in the end, as a group, we decided to base our scene on the news item. We all felt that the question of cyberbullying was something that many young people could identify with. This news item was just one of many that appeared in newspapers throughout the world. There were many questions we could try to convey through our devised piece. How are teenagers today cyberbullied? How can we prevent cyberbullying and what can we do to stay Cyber-safe? There were plenty of ideas for us to work on.

COMMENT ③
Remember to give reasons for your choice of stimulus.

2. Your choice of practitioner or genre. For your Unit 1 exam you were expected to include work on either the ideas and theories of a theatre practitioner or a genre of Theatre. Refer to any discussions within the group that took place before your final decision. Then state the name of your chosen practitioner or chosen genre. Briefly give a sentence or two about your chosen style/practitioner to show that you have studied them carefully before making your decision.

This is an example of a possible paragraph for this point:

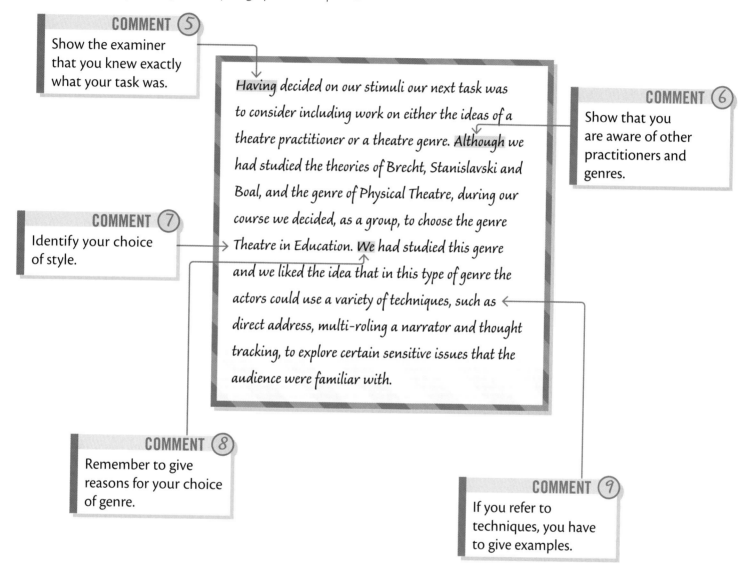

COMMENT 5
Show the examiner that you knew exactly what your task was.

COMMENT 6
Show that you are aware of other practitioners and genres.

COMMENT 7
Identify your choice of style.

COMMENT 8
Remember to give reasons for your choice of genre.

COMMENT 9
If you refer to techniques, you have to give examples.

Having decided on our stimuli our next task was to consider including work on either the ideas of a theatre practitioner or a theatre genre. Although we had studied the theories of Brecht, Stanislavski and Boal, and the genre of Physical Theatre, during our course we decided, as a group, to choose the genre Theatre in Education. We had studied this genre and we liked the idea that in this type of genre the actors could use a variety of techniques, such as direct address, multi-roling a narrator and thought tracking, to explore certain sensitive issues that the audience were familiar with.

3. You can go on to explain that a live performance you had seen had influenced you further in the choice of your genre:

COMMENT 10

Identify the name of the production that influenced you and the name of the production company that performed it.

COMMENT 11

Give a very brief summary – and I mean brief – of the story of the play you saw.

COMMENT 12

You must give reasons why this production made an impact on you.

> We were further influenced in our choice of genre by the live performance we saw by The Full House Theatre Company. Its title, 'Hope'. The play dealt with a range of issues that are currently facing young people, with a particular focus on web safety and cyberbullying. This performance made a definite impact on us. They made effective use of thought tracking, the dialogues were well written and the monologues engaged with us an audience. As a group we were very impressed by the way in which the monologues by the main character drew us in to the play. We decided to incorporate this technique in our devised work and I suggested that we each have a monologue to deliver to the audience. Throughout their performance they encouraged us as an audience to make our own decisions and judgements based on the scenarios they presented to us.

4. Your choice of theme and your contribution

You must now come to the theme of your devised scene. Give a brief summary of the story of your drama linking it up with your choice of stimuli and theatre genre. Refer to any contribution you made to the discussion.

COMMENT 13

Identify the theme of your devised piece.

COMMENT 14

Include any discussions you had as group regarding your chosen theme – and in this case, your target audience.

COMMENT 15

Show the examiner clearly what was your personal contribution to the discussions.

> After deciding on our stimulus and our style of production we then came to discuss the story of our drama. The theme of our play was obvious — cyberbullying, but the question we had to consider as a group was how to create a situation that dealt with this question in a sensitive manner and that posed questions to the audience to consider. We decided that our target audience would be Year 7 pupils. Therefore our story should be something that they could identify with and a story that, in the end, would educate them about this subject. We were 5 in the group but this didn't stop us from thinking of more characters since we could use the dramatic device of multi-roling. I suggested that we should start our performance with a narrator, introducing the audience to the main character. Again, following my suggestion, we decided that the main character was a girl who moved to a new school but soon found herself being cyberbullied.

COMMENT 16

DON'T waste time giving a long account of the storyline. Be brief!

Development

REMEMBER!!

This section carries the most marks and should include more detailed information

1. Make sure that the examiner knows your chosen skill – acting or technical.

2. Explain your choice of character and refer to the characters of others in the group.

3. Explain how you developed your character, referring to some of the strategies you used, such as hot seating.

Once we had decided upon our storyline we had to think of which characters we were going to use. My chosen skill for the project was acting and we decided that I would play the main character, Natalie. Owen was the only boy in the group, so we decided that he was to play the Head teacher and the boyfriend of one of Natalie's classmates. Catherine was to play the pupil who was responsible for the cyberbullying and Carey would be the narrator and one of Catherine's friends. The final member of the group was Nia and we decided that she would double up as Natalie's mother and one of the other classmates. I was chosen to play Natalie because I love playing emotional and dramatic roles and the character of Natalie would be a challenge because she was the one who was experiencing a very traumatic period in her life.

COMMENT 17
Refer to your chosen skill.

COMMENT 18
Identify your chosen character – and briefly refer to the other characters in your devised piece.

COMMENT 19
Give a good reason (or reasons) why you chose to play this particular character.

COMMENT 20

The examiner wants to know what strategies you used to develop your character. Give detailed examples.

In order to develop my character I did some research on the Internet and came across several stories about young people who had been cyberbullied. These stories made some very distressing reading and they showed quite clearly the emotional state of these victims, and led to the suicide of many of them.

We made use of the strategy of hot seating where the other members of the group asked me questions and I answered them in character, as Natalie. As a result of this work I realised that she had a real temper, she certainly didn't like being questioned about her relationship with the other girls – particularly her best friend. This information was really helpful because it meant that I could make the dialogue far more cutting and full of tension.

COMMENT 21

When referring to a strategy like 'hot seating' remember to say how this helped your development. You can also refer to other members in the group.

COMMENT 22

Watching a television programme dealing with the theme of your play is another strategy – or watching a live production. Again remember to say how this helped you in your development.

We did this with the other characters as well and this whole process really gave us deeper insights into our characters and helped us to depict them clearly to the audience. It certainly helped me realise how Natalie felt, what her emotional state was, what her feelings were towards the other members of the class and the relationship between her and her mother. Another strategy which helped me understand the character was watching an episode of 'Harry's Law' on television. This particular episode dealt with the question of a very serious case of cyberbullying and it showed, in conclusion, that everyone in situations like these needs help — the perpetrator, the victim and the families

I made notes about how my character should be communicated to the audience. My posture, expression and body language were very important in this respect. When we studied the genre of Physical Theatre we learnt how actors use movement, gesture and body language to show emotions or feelings, to convey different characters or to communicate their status to an audience. I would have to convey a very nervous and intimidated character and naturally my body language had to show this. I wouldn't be walking around with any confidence. My voice also would be rather quiet and I would talk slowly with plenty of pauses to show my nervousness and fear of the other members in the class. The dialogue between myself, as Natalie, and Catherine, as the bully, was quite a challenge to both of us. Catherine used a high pitched voice and her delivery of speech was sarcastic throughout. It was in this particular scene that Natalie realises the truth about the nasty texts sent to her and the vicious lies that were put on Facebook about her. My disbelief was expressed in just three simple words; 'It was you!' These words were said quietly and slowly and with feeling. My whole reaction was conveyed through body language and speech and I attempted to be a pitiful, nervous and oppressed victim, making sure, at the same time, that I did not over-exaggerate my actions.

COMMENT 23

It's important to show how you worked on communicating your character to the audience. Refer to use of body language, gestures, movements.

COMMENT 24

Remember that the use of voice is very important.

COMMENT 25

When referring to the use of movement and voice give examples of how you used these in communicating your character to the audience. It's always a good idea to give simple quotes from the scene.

4. Go on to show how the group developed ideas throughout the rehearsal period, e.g. did the structure of the devised work change? How? Did it improve?

5. What problems did you encounter? How did you overcome them?

COMMENT 26

The examiner will give extra marks if you refer to any practical work you did as a group during your rehearsal period.

Before we actually started writing our script we did a lot of improvisation work as a group to help us understand the characters and the different relationships. We improvised a scene between Natalie and Tracey, the girl who was bullying her. Another scene we improvised was a scene between Natalie and her mother. We explored the relationship between these two characters quite a lot. Did her mother realise what was happening to Natalie? What did the mother do when she realised what was happening to her daughter? We improvised a scene between the mother and the Head teacher. We used some of the ideas that arose during these improvisations in the final script.

COMMENT (27)

Refer to any difficulties you faced as a group during the rehearsal process.

COMMENT (28)

Show how you overcame these difficulties.

When we started rehearsing the scene some of the difficult aspects of the work were timing, maintaining characterisation and changing roles for those in the group playing more than one character. In order to overcome these difficulties we went back to the strategy of hot seating and each character in turn was questioned by the other members of the group. Timing was a big problem and some of us were delivering our words too quickly. The pace of many of the different scenes was too fast and we had to rehearse these over and over again in order to control the pace.

We felt that some of the scenes had to be very dramatic and powerful, especially between Natalie and Tracey, and between Natalie and her mother. An important scene was the one between Natalie's mother and the head teacher. This again was a dramatic scene especially when the mother realised that the head teacher had done nothing to help her daughter's situation. Nia, as the mother, shouted the words 'You knew and did nothing!', and Owen, as the head teacher, tried to justify his actions but could only stutter and reply 'I...I didn't... I thought...'.

COMMENT (29)

Again refer to a particular scene and give a quote from that scene.

COMMENT (30)

How did you improve the structure of your devised piece?

COMMENT (31)

Refer to any device which worked well in your opinion – and give a reason why.

When we were rehearsing these scenes we realised that we had too many bunched together and so we reworked and rearranged some of them and this improved the structure of our scene. What worked quite well with us was the device of cross-cutting – and this was most efficient when we had two different situations with Tracey and her friends and Tracey and Natalie – and it underlined that there are two sides to every story.

6. What strategies did you develop in rehearsal to show your chosen style or practitioner?

7. Give details of the acting area and any technical elements used.

In the TIE production we saw the use of pictures on a backdrop and the use of sound was brilliant and definitely made the play more dramatic. We did take photos of the group in character in different situations and used these in order to focus the audience's attention. We also underscored these photos with some emotional music and this proved to be very effective.

We chose to perform our play on a proscenium stage because this would allow us plenty of space and a minimalist set. Again coming back to the TIE production we saw we were very impressed by the way they created lots of different locations through simple objects. In addition to the projection of photos and the use of sound we used very simple lighting with some use of spotlights especially during the performance of some of the monologues.

COMMENT 32

Give examples of any technical elements you used and why these were effective in your opinion.

Link this to your chosen style.

COMMENT 33

Identify the type of acting area you chose – and give a reason why.

COMMENT 34

Refer to any sound or lighting used.

Performance

1. Evaluate your final performance and give some idea about audience feedback.

COMMENT 35

Give a brief introduction to the performance – a sentence or two.

The day of the exam arrived and 30 Year 7 pupils were actually going to watch our performance. Although we were all nervous performing in front of other pupils, we did think it was a good idea because at the end we knew that we would have feedback from them and this was important considering the genre we had chosen.

Carey as narrator in her introduction used her voice skills effectively, ensuring that pace, tone and voice level were correct and she indeed succeeded in gaining the audience's attention from the very beginning. The photos on the backdrop with the additional music worked well and this again made sure that the members of the audience were focused. I felt that my monologue at the beginning of the scene made an impact on the audience and hopefully I managed to engage with them. It was important for me to have voice control during this monologue. I wanted to establish my character and create a tense atmosphere and I think I achieved this by showing vocal variation, particularly in my pitch and volume, and the use of pauses. I also emphasised key words in the monologue. I was happy with what I achieved.

COMMENT 36

Give specific examples of any strengths and weaknesses in the final performance.

COMMENT 37

Show whether you felt the ideas presented in the rationale worked, or not.

Give an example of some good points.

As a group we felt that on the whole we interpreted the theme of cyberbullying quite effectively as it was evident throughout the performance that the audience were completely focused and that we had their attention from beginning to end. There were times also when I really felt as if I was truly experiencing the feelings of a victim of bullying since the interaction between Catherine, as the bully, and myself, was so believable. I also thought that each member of the group had thoroughly developed their characters and their final interpretation was truly effective.

COMMENT 38

Give an example (or examples) of some ideas that didn't work and show how you could resolve this issue in the future.

However, although some of the TIE techniques we used worked out quite well, I felt that the one example of thought tracking we tried was not as successful as we had hoped because the timing of speaking the thoughts of Natalie out loud by another member of the group was not perfect and it did not ring true. When attempting a similar technique in the future, I think that we should experiment further during the rehearsal process, with timing and the positioning of the characters on stage.

I was also aware that there were some examples of masking during the performance and this could have been avoided.

COMMENT 39

Refer to any audience response.

Our audience told us after the performance that they had enjoyed it and that the subject of our devised scene had a definite impact on them. Through our performance they had learnt a lot about the problem of cyberbullying and we had an opportunity to discuss with them a few of the questions we had discussed at the beginning of our project, namely, How can we prevent cyberbullying and what can we do to stay Cyber-safe? This proved to us that we had succeeded with our choice of style, namely TIE.

COMMENT 40

Show that you succeeded in your aim to educate and entertain your audience. Link it with your choice of style.

Now let's put all the sections together and the Evaluation should read like this:

Rationale

When we started our devised practical work our teacher gave us a selection of stimuli to choose from which would be the basis of our devised scene. We were shown a picture entitled Parsifal by the artist Anselm Kiefer, a news headline 'Teens arrested over Facebook Prank', the word Nightmare and a poem by Wilfred Owen, the war poet. We discussed each one in turn and could see possibilities in more than one of them but in the end, as a group, we decided to base our scene on the news item. We all felt that the question of cyberbullying was something that many young people could identify with. This news item was just one of many that appeared in newspapers throughout the world. There were many questions we could try to convey through our devised piece. How are teenagers today cyberbullied? How can we prevent cyberbullying and what can we do to stay Cyber-safe? There were plenty of ideas for us to work on.

Having decided on our stimuli our next task was to consider including work on either the ideas of a theatre practitioner or a theatre genre. Although we had studied the theories of Brecht, Stanislavski and Boal during our course we decided, as a group, to choose the genre Theatre in Education. We had studied this genre and we liked the idea that in this type of genre the actors could use a variety of techniques, such as direct address, multi-roling a narrator and thought tracking, to explore certain sensitive issues that the audience were familiar with.

We were further influenced in our choice of genre by the live performance we saw by The Full House Theatre Company. Its title, 'Hope'. The play dealt with a range of issues that are currently facing young people, with a particular focus on web safety and cyberbullying. This performance made a definite impact on us. They made effective use of thought tracking, the dialogues were well written and the monologues engaged with us an audience. As a group we were very impressed by the way in which the monologues by the main character drew us in to the play. We decided to incorporate this technique in our devised work and I suggested that we each have a monologue to deliver to the audience. Throughout their performance they encouraged us as an audience to make our own decisions and judgements based on the scenarios they presented to us.

After deciding on our stimulus and our style of production we then came to discuss the story of our drama. The theme of our play was obvious — cyberbullying, but the question we had to consider as a group was how to create a situation that dealt with this question in a sensitive manner and that posed questions to the audience to consider. We decided that our target audience would be Year 7 pupils. Therefore our story should be something that they could identify with and a story that, in the end, would educate them about this subject. We were 5 in the group but this didn't stop us from thinking of more characters since we could use the dramatic device of multi-roling. I suggested that we should start our performance with a narrator, introducing the audience to the main character. Again, following my suggestion, we decided that the main character was a girl who moved to a new school but soon found herself being cyberbullied.

Development

Once we had decided upon our storyline we had to think of which characters we were going to use. My chosen skill for the project was acting and we decided that I would play the main character, Natalie. Owen was the only boy in the group, so we decided that he was to play the head teacher and the boyfriend of one of Natalie's classmates. Catherine was to play the pupil who was responsible for the cyberbullying and Carey would be the narrator and one of Catherine's friends. The final member of the group was Nia and we decided that she would double up as Natalie's mother and one of the other classmates. I was chosen to play Natalie because I love playing emotional and dramatic roles and the character of Natalie would be a challenge because she was the one who was experiencing a very traumatic period in her life.

In order to develop my character I did some research on the Internet and came across several stories about young people who had been cyberbullied. These stories made some very distressing reading and they showed quite clearly the emotional state of these victims, and led to the suicide of many of them. We made use of the strategy of hot seating where the other members of the group asked me questions and I answered them in character, as Natalie. As a result of this work I realised that she had a real temper, she certainly didn't like being questioned about her relationship with the other girls — particularly her best friend. This information was really helpful because it meant that I could make the dialogue far more cutting and full of tension. We did this with the other characters as well and this whole process really gave us deeper insights into our characters and helped us to depict them clearly to the audience. It certainly helped me realise how Natalie felt, what her emotional state was, what her feelings were towards the other members of the class and the relationship between her and her mother. Another strategy which helped me understand the character was watching an episode of 'Harry's Law' on television. This particular episode dealt with the question of a very serious case of cyberbullying and it showed, in conclusion, that everyone in situations like these needs help — the perpetrator, the victim and the families.

I made notes about how my character should be communicated to the audience. My posture, expression and body language were very important in this respect. When we studied the genre of Physical Theatre we learnt how actors use movement, gesture and body language to show emotions or feelings, to convey different characters or to communicate their status to an audience. I would have to convey a very nervous and intimidated character and naturally my body language had to show this. I wouldn't be walking around with any confidence. My voice also would be rather quiet and I would talk slowly with plenty of pauses to show my nervousness and fear of the other members in the class. The dialogue between myself, as Natalie, and Catherine, as the bully, was quite a challenge to both of us. Catherine used a high pitched voice and her delivery of speech was sarcastic throughout. It was in this particular scene that Natalie realises the truth about the nasty texts sent to her and the vicious lies that were put on Facebook about her. My disbelief was expressed in just three simple words; 'It was you!' These words were said quietly and slowly and with feeling. My whole reaction to was conveyed through body language and speech and I attempted to be a pitiful, nervous and oppressed victim , making sure, at the same time, that I did not over-exaggerate my actions.

Before we actually started writing our script we did a lot of improvisation work as a group to help us understand the characters and the different relationships. We improvised a scene between Natalie and Tracey, the girl who was bullying her. Another scene we improvised was a scene between Natalie and her mother. We explored the relationship between these two characters quite a lot. Did her mother realise what was happening to Natalie? What did the mother do when she realised what was happening to her daughter? We improvised a scene between the mother and the head teacher. We used some of the ideas that arose during these improvisations in the final script.

When we started rehearsing the scene some of the difficult aspects of the work were timing, maintaining characterisation and changing roles for those in the group playing more than one character. In order to overcome these difficulties we went back to the strategy of hot seating and each character in turn was questioned by the other members of the group. Timing was a big problem and some of us were delivering our words too quickly. The pace of many of the different scenes was too fast and we had to rehearse these over and over again in order to control the pace. We felt that some of the scenes had to be very dramatic and powerful, especially between Natalie and Tracey, and between Natalie and her mother. An important scene was the one between Natalie's mother and the head teacher. This again was a dramatic scene especially when the mother realised that the head teacher had done nothing to help her daughter's situation. Nia, as the mother, shouted the words 'You knew and did nothing!', and Owen, as the head teacher, tried to justify his actions but could only stutter and reply 'I...I didn't... I thought...'. When we were rehearsing these scenes we realised that we had too many bunched together and so we reworked and rearranged some of them and this improved the structure of our scene. What worked quite well with us was the device of cross-cutting — and this was most efficient when we had two different situations with Tracey and her friends and Tracey and Natalie — and it underlined that there are two sides to every story.

In the TIE production we saw the use of pictures on a backdrop and the use of sound was brilliant and definitely made the play more dramatic. We did take photos of the group in character in different situations and used these in order to focus the audience's attention. We also underscored these photos with some emotional music and this proved to be very effective.

We chose to perform our play on a proscenium stage because this would allow us plenty of space and a minimalist set. Again, coming back to the TIE production we saw we were very impressed by the way they created lots of different locations through simple objects. In addition to the projection of photos and the use of sound we used very simple lighting with some use of spotlights especially during the performance of some of the monologues.

Performance

The day of the exam arrived and 30 Year 7 pupils were actually going to watch our performance. Although we were all nervous performing in front of other pupils, we did think it was a good idea because at the end we knew that we would have feedback from them and this was important considering the genre we had chosen.

Carey as narrator in her introduction used her voice skills effectively, ensuring that pace, tone and voice level were correct and she indeed succeeded in gaining the audience's attention from the very beginning. The photos on the backdrop with the additional music worked well and this again made sure that the members of the audience were focused. I felt that my monologue at the beginning of the scene made an impact on the audience and hopefully I managed to engage with them. It was important for me to have voice control during this monologue. I wanted to establish my character and create a tense atmosphere and I think I achieved this by showing vocal variation, particularly in my pitch and volume, and the use of pauses. I also emphasised key words in the monologue. I was happy with what I achieved.

As a group we felt that on the whole we interpreted the theme of cyberbullying quite effectively as it was evident throughout the performance that the audience were completely focused and that we had their attention from beginning to end. There were times also when I really felt as if I was truly experiencing the feelings of a victim of bullying since the interaction between Catherine, as the bully, and myself, was so believable. I also thought that each member of the group had thoroughly developed their characters and their final interpretation was truly effective.

However, although some of the TIE techniques we used worked out quite well, I felt that the one example of thought tracking we tried was not as successful as we had hoped because the timing of speaking the thoughts of Natalie out loud by another member of the group was not perfect and it did not ring true. When attempting a similar technique in the future, I think that we should experiment further during the rehearsal process, with timing and the positioning of the characters on stage.

I was also aware that there were some examples of masking during the performance and this could have been avoided.

Our audience told us after the performance that they had enjoyed it and that the subject of our devised scene had a definite impact on them. Through our performance they had learnt a lot about the problem of cyberbullying and we had an opportunity to discuss with them a few of the questions we had discussed at the beginning of our project, namely, How can we prevent cyberbullying and what can we do to stay Cyber-safe?

HOW TO EVALUATE

HOW TO WRITE AN EFFECTIVE EVALUATION

FOR EXAM PURPOSES

Always give reasons

Refer to your individual contribution

Always give good examples

Refer to strengths and areas for improvement during the devising process

Link to your chosen style: practitioner or genre

Include a few quotes from the devised scene

GLOSSARY

Allegorical – in the nature of an allegory (allegory – a play, picture, etc., in which the apparent meaning of the characters and events is used to symbolise a deeper moral or spiritual meaning).

Antagonist – opponent or adversary.

Atrocities – acts of extreme cruelty, especially against prisoners or civilians in wartime.

Body language – the gestures, postures, and facial expressions by which a person conveys various physical, mental, or emotional states and communicates non-verbally with others.

Burlesque – a theatrical entertainment of broad and earthy humour.

Characterisation – portraying a character on stage by imitating actions, gestures, or speeches.

Conscientious objector – a person who refuses to serve in the armed forces on the grounds of conscience.

Dilemma – a situation in which a difficult choice has to be made between two or more alternatives.

Ensemble acting – working as a group.

Freytag, Gustav – German novelist and playwright, famous for his 'Freytag Pyramid' i.e. where he explains a system for dramatic structure.

Gibberish – meaningless or unintelligible talk or writing; nonsense.

Impromptu – done without being planned or rehearsed.

Improvisations – to invent, compose, or perform with little or no preparation.

Integrity – honesty.

Interactive theatre – a theatrical form or work that breaks the 'fourth wall' that traditionally separates the performer from the audience both physically and verbally.

Involvement – the fact or condition of being involved with or participating in something.

Junta – a group of military officers ruling a country after seizing power.

Metaphorical – expressing one thing in terms normally denoting another.

Monotone speech – speech which is delivered on one note without change of pitch.

Narrator – person who tells a story.

Nuance – subtle difference in a meaning or feeling.

Opera – a theatrical presentation in which a dramatic performance is set to music.

Pathos – a feeling of sympathy or pity.

Physicalising – to express with the body.

Plot – the pattern of events or main story in a narrative or drama.

Protagonist – chief person in a play.

Rationale – rationales usually give reasons why a particular choice was made.

Scenario – a written outline of play giving details of the plot and individual scenes.

Stage directions – instructions to an actor or director, written into the script of a play.

Surrealistic – having an oddly dreamlike or unreal quality.

Vaudeville – a light comic play that often includes songs, pantomime, and dances.

Voice projection – the ability to make a sound heard at a distance.

Whimsical – fanciful, playful, joking.

BIBLIOGRAPHY

When I was researching for this book I came across some excellent books and resources dealing with some of the topics I wanted to include. I am indebted to some of these for giving me a clearer insight into the topics I wanted to discuss.

The Complete Stanislavski Toolkit Bella Merlin Nick Hern Books 2007
ISBN 978-1-85459-793-9

Stanislavski and the Actor Jean Benedetti Methuen Drama 1998
ISBN 978-1-4081-0686-0

Through the Body (A Practical Guide to Physical Theatre) Dymphna Callery Nick Hern Books 2001
ISBN 978-1-85459-638-7

Drama Games for Devising Jessica Swale Nick Hern Books 2012
ISBN 978-1-84842-037-3

Acting Skills Hugh Morrison A & C Black London 1992
ISBN 978-0-71366-423-2

Acting Through Song Paul Harvard Nick Hern Books 2013-06-17
ISBN 978-1-84842-229-2

Drama Yn Yr Ysgol Uwchradd Emyr Edwards CBAC 1998
ISBN 1-86085-325-0

Dyfeisio Theatr Emyr Edwards CBAC 2002
ISBN 1-86085-571-7

Devising (A Handbook for Drama and Theatre Students) Gill Lamden Hodder & Stoughton 2000
ISBN 0-340-78008-8

Games for Actors and Non-Actors Augusto Boal (Translated by Adrian Jackson) Routledge 2002
ISBN 0-415-26708-0

The Frantic Assembly Book of Devising Theatre Scott Graham & Steven Hoggett Routledge 2009
ISBN 978-0-415-46760-6

An excellent website:
Belgrade Community and Education Company www.belgrade.co.uk
Search for script resources and education packs.

INDEX

Photo credits:

P4 (& repeat on p20 & 29 & 39 & 96): Greatpapa/Shutterstock; GL Archive/Alamy; Interfoto/Alamy; AP/Press Association Images; P5: Leszek Glasner/Shutterstock; P6: Geraint Lewis/Alamy; Featureflash/Shutterstock; Geraint Lewis/Alamy; P7: Alexsandr Sulga; P8: LSQRD42/Shutterstock; P9:kldy/Shutterstock; Nordicphotos/Alamy; Korionov/Shutterstock; Everett Collection/Shutterstock; P13: AF Archive/Alamy CBS; P14 David Stock/Alamy; Paul David Drabble/Alamy; Twin Design/Shutterstock; P15 Sheli Jensen/Shutterstock; P17: 1000 Words/Shutterstock; P18: Ruth Black/Shutterstock; P22 Silent Scream John Timbers/ArenaPAL; P23 Donald Cooper/Photostage, info@photostage.co.uk; P24: Frank Wasserfuehrer/ Shutterstock; P25: The Print Collector/Alamy; P26: Pictorial Press Ltd/Alamy; P27: Parable of the Blind (tempera on canvas) Bruegel, Pieter the Elder (c.1525–69)/Museo e Gallerie Nazionali di Capodimonte, Naples, Italy/Giraudon/The Bridgeman Art Library; P28: ollirg/Shutterstock; P31: AF Archive/Alamy United Artists; P32: Surijeta/Shutterstock; P33: The Art Gallery Collection/Alamy; P35 David Davis/Shutterstock; Anton Balazh/Shutterstock; P38: Leah-Anne Thompson; p39: Corbis All Rights Reserved; P41: Ed Swinden; P42: Getty Images; P43: Jonathan McIntosh; P45: Robodread/Shutterstock; P Burton Images; P47 AHTuner/Shutterstock; p48: Belgrade Theatre, Coventry; P49: CragRats (UK) Limited; GAZEBO Theatre in Education Company; Theatr na nOg; P50: Keith Moris; P51: Bitesize Theatre Co, Wrexham, North Wales, bitesizetheatre.co.uk; P53: Ljupco Smokovski/ Shutterstock; Andy Dean Photography/Shutterstock; P54: Homer Sykes Archive/Alamy; p57: Trevor Smith/Alamy; P61: Ana Blazic Pavlovic/Shutterstock; Real Deal Photography/Shutterstock; Andrey Shadrin/Shutterstock; P62: Wrangler/Shutterstock; William Perugini/Shutterstock; P64: Mandy Godbehear/Shutterstock; P65: Christian Bertrand/ Shutterstock; P67: MegainArmy/Shutterstock; Arthur van der Kooij/Shutterstock; JetKat/Shutterstock; Seleznev Oleg/Shutterstock; LeonP/Shutterstock; Suranga Weeratunga/Shutterstock; P68: Ljupco Smokovski; P69: Alain Chambaretaud; P70: Getty Images/Keith Brofsky; P71: Vladimir Nikitin/Shutterstock; Christian Bertrand/Shutterstock; P72: The Frantic Assembly Book of Devising Theatre, Scott Graham and Steven Hoggett, © 2009 Routledge. Reproduced by permission of Taylor & Francis Books UK; P73: p73 (r) lassedesign-Fotolia.com; P74: Samuel Borges Photography/Shutterstock; P75: Kids R Us/Emma Holmes Channel; UK Productions Ltd; P76: Bill Kenwright Ltd; Littlestar; P77: Paul Doyle/Alamy; Theatrepix/Alamy; Paul Doyle/Alamy; P78: Pozyakov/Shutterstock; P79: Tate, London 2013; P81: © Jeff Morgan 03 / Alamy; P83: S_Bukley/Shutterstock; P84: Susan Law Cain/Shutterstock; P85: Mandy Godbehear/Shutterstock; P86: Lebedinski Vladislav/Shutterstock; Boyan Dimitrov/Shutterstock; P87: Christopher Halloran/Shutterstock; P88: Walter Wykes; P89: Photos 12/Alamy; P91: AF Archive/Alamy; P92: Sebastian Gauert/Shutterstock; P93: Pavel L Photo & Video/Shutterstock; P94: Iakov Filimonov

Text Permissions:

P7: Drama Games for Devising by Jessica Swale, © 2012 Nick Hern Books, www.nickhernbooks.co.uk; P11: Cuba by Liz Lochhead, published as Cuba & Dog House by Liz Lochhead and Gina Moxley, Faber, 2000; P12: Effie's Burning by Valerie Windsor, published by Samuel French Ltd, 1995; P13: Death of a Salesman by Arthur Miller, published by Penguin Classics (New Ed) 2000; P37 Exercises adapted from ideas in both Stanislavski and the Actor: The Method of Physical Action, Jean Benedetti and published by Routledge 1998, and The Complete Stanislavski Toolkit by Bella Merlin, published by Nick Hern Books, 2007; P44: Games for Actors and Non Actors by Augusto Boal (trans. Adrian Jackson), published by Routledge 2002; P55 (& part p62/3): The Last Heroes by Nick Walker, written by Nick Walker as part of the Belgrade Theatre Community and Education Company HLF Project, 2008. Other exercises adapted from the same pack. P72–3: The Frantic Assembly book of Devising Theatre, Scott Graham and Steven Hoggett, published by Routledge, 2009; P81: Disco Inferno/Justin Sepple, © 2004 by Justin Sepple, reproduced by permission of Josef Weinberger Ltd on behalf of David Spicer Productions; P84: Waste by Studdert Kennedy, published by Hodder & Stoughton 1929; P88 The Worker © 2007 by Walter Wykes. Inquiries concerning all rights for this play should be directed to the playwright at sandmaster@aol.com; p92/3 Exercises adapted from the Active8 theatre website, active8theatre@googlemail.com